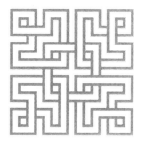

DANTE'S PATH

Vulnerability and the Spiritual Journey

Bonney Gulino Schaub, RN, MS
Richard Schaub, PhD

Florence Press

D1714572

ISBN 978-0692276853

By Bonney Gulino Schaub and Richard Schaub
schaub@huntingtonmeditation.com
www.florencepress.com
www.huntingtonmeditation.com

Cover photo by George Schaub
All interior photos by George Schaub
Book design by Aericon.com
Back photo by Kerry St. Ours

Florence Press

Original title: Dante's Path: A Practical Approach to Achieving Inner Wisdom
Published by Penguin Putnam, 2003

Second edition: Dante's Path: Vulnerability and the Spiritual Journey
Published by Florence Press, 2014. (www.FlorencePress.com)

Excerpts from Dante: The Divine Comedy. Volume 1: Inferno, Volume II: Purgatory, Volume III: Paradise, translated by Mark Musa, used by permission of Indiana University Press

Anonymous church poem translated by Susie Rosselli and used by permission of Susie Rosselli

Meditation exercises from Healing Addictions: The Vulnerability Model of Recovery, published by Delmar, 1997. Copyright by Bonney Gulino Schaub and Richard Schaub

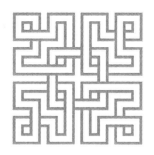

To

Kurt Andrew, Aisha Krista, Marisol,
Lucinda Rose, Ava Grace, Fiona Hope

and future generations

Contents

CHAPTER SIX

CHAPTER SEVEN

CHAPTER EIGHT

CHAPTER NINE

LIST OF EXERCISES

INTRODUCTION TO
SECOND EDITION

Dante mapped the classic Western spiritual journey. It is as relevant and potent for you today as it was during Dante's time (14th Century) because it is about discovering the highest possibilities in your nature.

We first wrote *Dante's Path* to help bring Dante's wisdom and inspiration to the modern reader, and Penguin Putnam published it right after the destruction of September 11, 2001 for that same reason. Oprah's book, Live Your Best Life, generously featured the book and our work as "divine therapy."

By 2003, *Dante's Path* had generated letters from around the world, including priests, ministers, rabbis and imams, American soldiers in Iraq, spiritual seekers of every background, and some people trying to get out of hell, including hospitals and prisons. Once you understand Dante's stated intention ("to help future generations to move from misery to bliss"), you grasp the power of the work. This second edition is being published by our own press, Florence Press, in response to many requests to make the book available again.

Nothing in human nature has substantially changed since Dante wrote in 1307. His insight that "because people suffer, they make other people suffer" remains true – and unsolved. How do you solve suffering? There actually is a path. You go on a journey inside yourself and awaken your highest potentials for wisdom, illumination and oneness. These potentials objectively exist, and in this book we show you the path by connecting you to one of the world's great spiritual guides, the Florentine poet Dante.

A note about the photographs. We didn't have images in the first edition. Our imagery choice for this second edition is mostly modern street scenes to emphasize the present-moment importance of Dante's message. The nature photographs are, of course, eternal.

Bonney Gulino Schaub
Richard Schaub

Florence Press

Huntington NY,
September 2014

The Experience Of More

You have within you all the potential for a special relationship that is waiting to be realized right now. It is the relationship between your everyday personality and a deep source of internal wisdom. Sometimes, at night, you might experience this wisdom as knowledge or guidance you receive in your dreams. Sometimes, during the day, a word or phrase or passing mental image might indicate that your internal wisdom is trying to get through to your conscious self. And, on some occasions, in a moment of true grace, a big piece of internal wisdom might break through to your awareness and illuminate reality more fully than you had ever seen it before.

Around the world and throughout the ages, people have been searching for ways to access this internal wisdom in order to experience the benefits it has to bestow. Tapping into that wisdom will reveal your purpose for living, your destiny, and with that new understanding your fears will relax, the right choices about the directions of your life will become obvious, you will live with greater peace, and more love will flow to and from your mind and heart.

There are many names for this deep source of wisdom. It is the mystic's vision, the artist's muse, the scientist's intuition. The Old Testament prophets received it by seeing visions and hearing voices: Elijah referred to it as "the still small voice within," and when Moses ascended the mountain to receive wisdom about how to lead his people and asked for a name by which to call the source of his guidance, he was told only, "Tell them that 'I Am' sent you." Tibetan Buddhists call this internal wisdom *prajna*. The Zen tradition refers to the "inner reason of the universe which exists in each mind." Gandhi meditated in order to receive guidance from what he called "the inner light" of universal truth. The *Kabbalah* of the Jewish mystics call this higher center of wisdom the *Tiferet*, and Greek mythology speaks of it as the oracle. In the 12 Steps of

Alcoholics Anonymous it is the "Higher Power."

Dante, in *The Divine Comedy*, his masterful poetic description of spiritual seeking, personified inner wisdom as his female guide, Beatrice. Carl Jung referred to it as "the Self." And our own teacher, Dr. Roberto Assagioli, called it the "higher self" and founded a school of modern psychology, which he called psychosynthesis, to develop a human science of the higher self because it was his belief, as it is ours, that access to this higher self could be studied and taught as a practical, scientific fact. We have come to call it the "wisdom mind" in order to distinguish it from the rational mind in our discussions with patients and students.

To know that this higher aspect of yourself exists and is available to you is certainly good news. The problem, however, is that this may be the first time anyone has told you about it. In order to form a relationship, you must first become acquainted with the other party — in this case your own inner wisdom — and then begin to nourish the bond between you. The purpose of this book is to help you do just that — to educate you about this higher part of your nature and teach you how to be in relationship with it so that you, too, can enjoy its life-changing benefits in the course of your daily life.

The path to forming a relationship with your wisdom mind is not magical or mysterious. Rather, it is a creative process in which, through a series of discoveries, your experience of who you are is gradually expanded. You begin exactly as you are, stay exactly who you are, and, simultaneously, you become *more*. Your core personality doesn't change; you still function as "you" in the world and in your relationships with others on a daily basis, but you also begin to notice yourself gaining more perspective and purpose and feeling more at peace. "Reality" is no longer just the version presented to you by social convention — a life of surviving, functioning, and then relaxing from surviving and functioning. Rather, you will also begin to experience the deeper reality that the saints and mystics have always told us about — those moments of wisdom and illumination in which you see into the underlying harmonious order of life. You won't transcend everyday reality; you'll still live out your life like everyone else, but you'll live it with an awareness of belonging to a greater life that you can trust.

Personally, we each trace our own curiosity about the nature of this inner wisdom to a particular early experience. Richard's occurred when, at the age of nineteen, he was lying in spiritual bliss in a tiny, pitch-black, soundproof room in the basement of a Princeton University building as a subject in a study of sensory deprivation being done for the United States Navy Astronaut Research. Bonney's occurred when she was just thirteen, sitting in a state of transcendent joy while staring at Monet's Water Lilies in the Museum of Modern Art in New York City. While both of us remember even earlier breakthrough experiences of inner wisdom, these events were the conscious turning points at which we became aware of a deeper potential hidden within human nature.

Professionally, we have investigated the human potential for wisdom and illumination through the field of transpersonal ("beyond personality") psychology, which studies the integration of personality and spirituality. Developed in the United States in the 1960s, transpersonal psychology has its roots in the work of two European psychiatrists, Carl Jung and Roberto Assagioli. They were both students of Sigmund Freud, but they broke away from his psychoanalytic movement because of its failure to address the spiritual aspect of human nature.

We discovered Assagioli's first book, *Psychosynthesis,* when we were searching for a source of psychotherapy training that included a spiritual component, and we immediately felt at home with his thinking. What impressed us most deeply was his brutally realistic view of the darkness and difficulties of life and the fact that his own commitment to studying the higher potentials in human nature was actually strengthened during a very low and dark period in his life.

Assagioli was born in the Jewish ghetto in Venice in 1888. Having lived through the loss of both parents by the time he was a teenager, he was guided by his stepfather, a physician, to become a psychiatrist and student of psychoanalysis. In 1909, he was named the Italian representative to the Vienna Psychoanalytic Society, founded by Freud, the then-still-controversial father of psychoanalysis. Assagioli studied for a time in Switzerland, at the same hospital as Jung, but quickly became dissatisfied with psychoanalysis because, for him, it ignored the healthier possibilities inherent in human nature, including higher consciousness and spirituality. At the age of only twenty-two, he broke with the psychoanalytic movement and began to formulate his own method of practicing psychotherapy, founding the first institute for teaching psychosynthesis in Rome in 1928.

In 1940 he was labeled a pacifist and imprisoned by the Fascists. Instead of breaking him, however, his imprisonment provided Assagioli with what he termed "a blessing":

...the realization of independence from circumstances, the realization of inner freedom. We should realize the freedoms from fear, want, etc., but the right emphasis should be given that inner freedom without which all others are not sufficient. My dedication is going to be to the task of helping men and women free themselves from inner prisons...

Friends finally secured Assagioli's release, but his troubles were far from over. He remained under strict police scrutiny and, with the advent of the Nazi occupation, was forced into hiding in the Tuscan hills. Shortly after the war, his only child died from an illness he developed while the family was in hiding. It was not until 1950 that Assagioli was able to reopen the psychosynthesis institute, this time in Florence.

Assagioli was the first modern Western doctor to incorporate worldwide spiritual and meditative practices directly into his work with patients. By the late 1950s, word of his approach had spread, professionals from around the world began to seek him out as a teacher, and, since that time, many others have begun to emphasize the importance of integrating spirituality into the paradigm for seeking mental and emotional health.

But if our teacher was Roberto Assagioli, you may well be asking by now, why have we called our book about the educational and creative process of connecting with inner wisdom *Dante's Path* rather than Assagioli's? The answer is that Assagioli's own path actually led him back to the work of the 14th - century poet-mystic Dante Alighieri. Like so many of his countrymen, Assagioli had studied Dante's poetic masterpiece, *The Divine Comedy*, in which Dante's alter-ego, the pilgrim, goes on a spiritual journey through the realms of hell, purgatory, and paradise. In Assagioli's case, however, that study went well beyond the literary to become a formidable influence on his own work.

For Assagioli, Dante was a spiritual sage who had, in his poem, mapped the entire course of the spiritual path Assagioli himself had traveled and along which he was guiding his patients. In his notes on the suffering of his psychiatric patients, he refers again and again to Dante's hell. In his notes on people's struggles to live with less fear and more freedom, he refers to Dante's purgatory. And in his references to spiritual states of being, he speaks of the poet's paradise. Dante had, in fact, visited all the realms of human experience and discovered both the worst and the best in human nature. For the modern psychiatrist, the visionary poet was a realistic teacher of enlightenment who had, six hundred years before Assagioli's commitment to freeing others from their inner prisons, dedicated his own work to leading future generations "from misery to bliss." Dante paints a brilliantly illuminative word picture not only of the states of misery and bliss but also of the sometimes difficult path we must travel on our journey from one to the other, and Assagioli supplies both the modern understanding of human psychology and the practical methods available to us for having direct experiences of our natural higher potentials.

As psychotherapists and teachers of other health professionals, we emphasize the lifelong *practicality* of following this path to the realization of wisdom and illumination because, in our thirty years of practice, we've found that many of the problems we all have as human beings cannot be solved simply by rearranging the furniture of our personal and professional relationships. Many of our problems function as disguises for the real problem — our knowledge that we are but temporary citizens of life and that everyone and everything we see passes away. This is a fact everyone would prefer to deny, and yet, much of the fear, worry, doubt, and anger we live with on a daily basis flows inexorably from its unalterable truth. Our promise to you is that, by following the path we have traveled in the footsteps of Dante and Assagioli, and that we will map for you in the pages that follow, you, too, will be able to find a way of relaxing the grip of your fears and deepening your awareness of your intimate connection to the whole of the harmonious, eternal, interpenetrating, mysterious universe. It is a transformation everyone, including you, is capable of achieving, and your way of accomplishing it is by developing an ongoing relationship with your guiding internal wisdom.

In addition to making this promise, however, we also recognize the importance of acknowledging the obstacles that block many of us from realizing this innate, universal potential. All these obstacles, as you will learn, are really forms of fear. Fear has many faces, some of the more obvious of which are anxiety, insecurity, hurt, and worry. It can, however, also be disguised as anger, greed, envy, negativity, addiction, betrayal, or violence. Using Dante's map of hell as a guide, we will lead you on a tour of all our shared human fears so that you will be able to recognize those that are most prevalent in your own life. And, once you've gained that self-knowledge, we'll teach you safe, effective, time-tested methods of liberating yourself from your fears each time they threaten to block your progress.

The methods Assagioli used in his practice, and that we use with our own patients, are forms of applied meditation and imagery that you, too, can use everyday. As you practice them yourself, you will begin to experience more and more liberation from fear, and, with the quieting of your fears, you will become better able to hear the subtle voice of your wisdom mind. We will then guide you to develop and strengthen your relationship with that higher part of your nature so that its benefits will gradually be able to flow more and more freely.

Inspired by Dante and Assagioli, we had been thinking about writing this book of practical spirituality for many years when the events of September 11, 2001, motivated us to finally put our thoughts into action. Tragedy, as we had already learned all too well, is often the catalyst that moves people to become spiritual seekers. We had been working with the therapeutic uses of imagery and meditation for many years when, in the 1980s, we began to see, both in our practices and in our community service work, more and more people who were either dying of AIDS or losing friends and loved ones to that dreadful disease. And, over and over, we saw our patients reviewing the meaning of their lives and searching for the spiritual strength to cope with their devastation. These people were truly in a "hellish" state, and they were suddenly struck by the realization that whatever material success they might have achieved, it was no more than temporary. They required some deeper inner wisdom or spiritual awareness to comfort them and give them courage.

We have also worked at various points in our careers in medical centers and drug and alcohol treatment agencies and have seen many forms of suffering that required us to help people draw down deep into themselves for strength. But hellish states, suffering, and the desire for deeper wisdom are not the sole property of people with frightening illnesses. We have also been therapists for hundreds of people who are simply discontent with their life as it is, people who have come to believe there must be something "more" to life than what they are experiencing but who don't know how or where to find it—people who are, perhaps, very much like you.

Finally, going beyond these clinical experiences, we have had the joy of leading groups of people on several Sacred Art Tours of Florence during which we were able to introduce them to the universal spiritual wisdom embodied in Renaissance art and teach them how to practice visualization meditation as they sat before those sacred paintings. Having witnessed the illuminations experienced by so many of our travelers during their meditation, we became more convinced than ever that the tools for touching and tasting deeper wisdom were, quite literally, right in front of our eyes.

With this book we will guide you, as we have our patients, our students, and our Florentine travelers, on your own journey to discovering your inner wisdom. As both fellow seekers and spiritual scouts, we offer you not only a map to make the trip less confusing, but also a clear promise of the transformational rewards it will bring.

CHAPTER ONE
Maps And Guides

The Divine Comedy is imbued with the universally held religious beliefs of 14th - century Italy, which have made the timeless truths it conveys difficult for some readers to recognize. These days, some countries may have a predominant or even an "official" religion, but most people are free to espouse whatever belief system they choose, or none at all. Our students and patients come to us with a virtually endless variety of beliefs (or non-beliefs), their one unifying characteristic being that none so far has found a way to satisfy his or her need for connection with the spirituality he senses is lacking in his life.

Personally, we have traveled many paths before stumbling upon the road that ultimately took us to the self-development practices and spiritual perspective we benefit from now. Like many others, we had followed a traditional, inherited religion; we had given up belief in anything at all for the cynical belief in nothing; and we had tried cobbling together a selection of teachings from various sources to construct a belief system we hoped would be unique to our needs. Each one of these paths, however, presented a different kind of roadblock. Believing in what others had said did not lead to our own experiences or to new development. The cynical belief in nothing violated our desire to know more and closed our minds to other possibilities. And belief in our own patchwork construction always seemed suspect even to us — did we really know what we were talking about?

Finally, we came to approach our spiritual search in a practical way. We began to test a variety of spiritual maps and guides with one simple, elegant question: Does it work? "Working," for us, meant helping us to live our lives with more love and less fear.

The kind of love we are speaking about here is not romantic attraction or loving conditionally because the object of your love provides you with something specific that you want or need. We mean the love that is a universal, ever-present, indestructible reality to be fully touched and tasted in the course of mystical discovery but also sensed in even the most humble behaviors of daily life. When you unite with that love, even for a moment—in a relationship, in a work of art, or in a ray of light—its unique quality moves through your entire mind, body, and mood, and when you merge with it, as Dante's Pilgrim did, you come back changed forever.

Although we may not consciously realize what exactly it is we seek, we all, on some level, yearn for this merging, this greater love that will wash away our fears and negativities and make the world right again. One thing the founders of all our Western Judeo-Christian-Islamic traditions had in common was their personal experience of mystical breakthroughs that took them into direct contact with the energy of love that, they have taught, is at the core of our reality and the point of our living.

Finding Our Guide

Our own search for "what worked" culminated in our discovery of a wise guide, Roberto Assagioli, whose own seeking has provided our map every since. Assagioli himself had tried many systems, many methods, many paths, and had corresponded or visited with spiritual teachers and philosophers around the world. Initially, we were intrigued by the fact that he was both a highly educated and scientifically trained Western medical professional and one who was at home in the world of spiritual literature, spiritual seeking, and spiritual experiences. Following his path has allowed us to honor our scientific thinking and common sense while at the same time we explore higher states of consciousness in order to see what we might learn.

Most spiritual thinkers and authors of spiritual literature

advocate that in order to deepen your spirituality you must first get rid of your ego (or, even more extreme, that the very notion of *self* is an illusion). That concept had never seemed practical to us; in other words, it didn't work. If we got rid of our ego, the part of our mind that organizes our multitudinous thoughts and feelings into coherent, intentional actions, we would not be able to focus ourselves well enough to function at work, earn money, and feed our children. Unless we were willing to surrender our autonomy and individuality by joining some kind of commune or cult, so long as we chose instead to continue living in the real world, how were we to pay the rent? Addressing this issue, Assagioli put it very simply by saying, "The human ego is part of a higher organizing process in nature, and so the idea of getting rid of it is silly."

That view seemed to us extremely realistic and based on common sense. The path to spiritual and personal development that he proposed was an open - ended process rather than a specific program that required us to follow rigidly laid down patterns of thought. Assagoli saw spirituality as a natural part of our basic humanity, equal to, but not more important than our physical biology and our social personality. In his view, our biology, our personality, and our spirituality *together* comprise the basic elements of our nature, and each of those components has its own needs and demands. According to that view, our physical and emotional health requires that we respond to the needs of all three. And, in his opinion, it was the education and exploration of our spiritual self that had been the most neglected element of our nature, and the one around which much ignorance and superstition had gathered.

Assagioli's Map of Human Nature

Assagioli formulated a map of our biological-social-spiritual nature that has worked for us. It has, in other words, allowed us to live with more love and less fear without trying to deny or suppress any part of ourselves. We have also used Assagioli's map, as he did, to do psychotherapeutic work that honors the higher needs and possibilities of our students and patients while also recognizing their very real fears and conflicts. By doing that, we have been able to help hundreds of people, and we offer that map to you here as a way to start you on your own journey.

Your biological self is dominated by the need to survive. It wants you to use your attention to look for signs of danger and/or threat taking place either in your body or in the environment. It wants you to worry, to plan carefully so that nothing will go wrong, to get angry and territorial about even the simplest conflicts, to fantasize escape, to think only of yourself, and to be suspicious, even paranoid, about other people as a way of staying prepared. In other words, your biological self wants you to control every aspect of life, and, as a result, it sends you fight-or-flight signals all day long, even about situations that are not really dangerous.

Your social self is dominated by the need to belong, to be approved of, and so it wants you to use your attention to evaluate situations according to whether you are included or excluded. It wants you to compare yourself to others, to judge others, to deflate others and to inflate yourself, to look for opportunities to win more approval, reward, status, or self-esteem, and to adjust your thoughts and behavior so that you can win those things. Like your biological self, your social self fights for survival, but it is the survival of your self-image that is its driving need. It sends you signals of self-consciousness and self-absorption to keep you on track toward satisfying its need.

Your spiritual self is of an entirely different dimension because it is not concerned with the survival of either your body or your self-image. Your spiritual self is connected to creation itself. It knows that all things come and go as part of the natural cycle, and it is at peace with that obvious fact of life. As part of its connection to creation, your spiritual self is dominated by the need to take care of life, to take care of creation, to fulfill your part, your purpose, while you are here. The most human manifestation of this caring for life is being loving, and Mary, Kuan Yin, the Shehinah aspect of God and other universal symbols are all expressions of this love that is rooted in creation itself.

Your spiritual self wants you to fulfill that loving purpose, and so it tries to keep your attention on its truth and prevent you from getting too lost in false purposes. It is not uncommon for people to misdirect their innate spiritual impulse toward achieving some social goal such as gaining more approval or higher status, and then, when they have reached that goal, to still feel no lasting sense of fulfillment or peace. One of our patients, for example, talked to us about having won an Academy Award and awakening the following morning to a feeling of emptiness. Another described the moment he stared for the first time at his just-completed, huge, expensive home and thought, "And now what?" Both these people had lost their true purpose without even realizing it until they recognized what little meaning their social accomplishments actually held for them.

Just as your biological self sends you fight-or-flight signals, and your social self sends signals of self-consciousness and self-absorption, your spiritual self has its own signals: It sends you a feeling of longing, of missing out, when you are living too disconnected from your purpose, and the signal to start searching again when you have gotten too far from the truth.

As you can see, each of these three elements of your nature wants something different from you, and each wants you to focus specifically on its particular needs. Your attention is constantly being pulled in different directions, and so, when you feel "all over the place"—as many people tell us they do—it is because you are. The elements of your very nature are in active competition with one another. All of their needs are undeniable, and all need to be met. The question then becomes how to coordinate them as best we can, so that we can live with as much internal harmony as possible.

Discovering Dante

Assagioli died in 1974, and we never got to meet him. But in 1990, after many years of studying and then teaching his work, we felt irresistibly drawn to deepen the bond we already felt with him by visiting his home city of Florence, where his papers are archived. We were both self-employed, and we couldn't really afford to take the time off from work, but we knew we had to go—for us it felt like a pilgrimage—and so we went, determined to stay for a month.

The very day we arrived, we went where all the tourists in Florence go—to the Duomo (Santa Maria del Fiore, the main cathedral). Crowds pour in through the door on the right and out through the door on the left, but the inner vastness of the Duomo dwarfs all human activity. In such a magnificent space, you wonder where to look first. Our immediate instinct was to go toward a large painting on a side wall, and the result of that fortuitous choice has been both many years of study and the writing of this book.

The painting was di Michelino's "*Dante and his Poem.*" It shows the sage and poet Dante holding his poem, *The Divine Comedy*, while depicted around him are the three realms of the journey— descending to hell , climbing the mountain of purgatory, and entering into paradise.

We stared at Dante. He stared back at us. He seemed to be saying: "Here is the map of all the human worlds. Take the journey and discover what I found." We felt a deep and immediate emotional connection with that painting but did not yet understand its source.

Two weeks later, we were sitting in the library archives of Assagioli's home in Florence. We had come to Florence because we had instinctively felt the need to be closer to the teacher we had never met. We had called to request access to the library as soon as we arrived, but we had also been told that a previous American student had stolen from the archives and so we knew there was a good chance we would not be allowed in. For several days we got no reply, but then, out of the blue, the library secretary returned our call, and we made an appointment to meet her.

We spoke to her in simple, bad Italian, and she graciously spoke back to us in a few words of hesitant English. Then, in the middle of the conversation, she smiled, turned around, and got us the key. Perhaps our gratitude for Assagioli's work had come through to her.

We returned to that small, sunny library again and again. As we read Assagioli's intimate notes about his early work, his imprisonment by the Fascists, the death of his son, his spiritual experiences, his scholarly explorations, his search for practical methods to help his patients, we began to feel deeply attached to him and privileged to have access to his handwritten thoughts and feelings in a place so imbued with his gentle spirit.

Assagioli had read books in five languages (Italian, French, German, English and Sanskrit) and had written notes in all but Sanskrit, which made many of them difficult for us to read. We discovered, however, that in his later years, once people from around the world began to seek him out, his notes were increasingly written in English. He referred to many mystics, artists, saints, philosophers, poets and political thinkers, and he was always trying to synthesize these sources. As his work continued, he arrived at a way of being, an openness to higher consciousness, that brought him increasingly frequent experiences of illumination. Again and again in his notes we found brief jottings that said simply, "Joy, overflowing joy," "*Gioia,*" or "Silent joy."

One day, we were talking with a former student of his, now a doctor in Florence, about our research, when he suddenly asked, rubbing his fingers together, "Can you feel the joy?" To this day, many years after Assagioli's death, his students, now psychiatrists and psychologists all over Italy, still become animated with humor and gratitude when they talk about him.

It was in going through Assagioli's notes that we discovered his deep identification with Dante. Not only with the literary Dante of the Duomo painting or the Dante of the spiritual journey to hell, purgatory, and paradise described in *The Divine Comedy*, but with the Dante who, despite a life of exile and loss, had emerged as a purposeful and enlightened teacher.

When we returned from Florence, we plunged immediately into an intensive study of Dante and his poem. We read *The Divine Comedy* many times in many translations and slowly began to get past the obstacles to understanding presented by his 14th-century historical, literary, and religious references. We began to see that Dante's hell was a catalogue of our fears, his passage through purgatory was the road to liberation from those fears, and paradise was the realm in which we explore higher consciousness.

To Make It Real, Begin in Hell

Dante took one third of *The Divine Comedy* to describe in painful detail all of the hell impulses in human nature—indifference, lust, addiction, greed, rage, pride, violence, fraud, betrayal—behaviors that were described as "sins" in the Middle Ages but are behaviors we still engage in and encounter every day—at home, at work, in our neighborhood, our nation and in our world.

Hell is a place we want to get out of. It's old news. We hear about it in our daily papers and on the nightly news. It is in our city, in our town. People hate one another, betray one another, and kill one another. They are stupid, addicted, obsessive, and unbelievably insensitive. They are full of rage or pride. They cheat and lie—and on and on. Our history books contain stories of slaughter told side by side with accounts of the advances and discoveries of creative humanity. Scientists discover how to split the atom and then use that knowledge to build the most destructive bomb the world has ever known. We just cannot seem to keep hell out of our behavior.

The relevance of Dante's exploration of hell is brought home to us again and again as despairing clients who have been through hellish experiences ask, "What's wrong with people? How can they do this to each other? Where is God in all of this? If God exists, and He let this happen, then I hate Him." The recurrence of hell in human affairs makes us all doubt humanity's long-term chances for survival. But the very fact that it is so ubiquitous is actually the reason that our spiritual journey needs to include the exploration of this darkness. Because, if hell is all around us, the answers we arrive at will be required to hold up in the face of the pain, suffering, and loss we encounter every day.

The challenge is: How can we love the whole thing? It does not seem possible, since the full cycle of life—birth, growth, decay, and death—is not itself lovable. Birth and growth are easy to love, but decay and death are easy to fear. One half of life is lovely while the other is fearful. Fear is planted firmly in the middle of our existence. It seems that nothing can change it. Throw what you will at it—art, religion, science; fear just swallows them up and stares back at us. It just is. It is an eternal state.

Start with Fear

That is why Dante's acknowledgment of hell is, in a way, so reassuring. His very humanity, all his questions, doubts, fears, and emotional reactions are incorporated into the map he draws for finding states of higher consciousness and harmony in living.

Have you ever seen one of those maps of a public transportation system that indicate with an X or a circle "You are here"? That's what Dante does. He tells us that we must start from wherever we are. We do not have to suppress our emotions in order to be more spiritual, and we do not need to suppress our mind in order to have no thoughts or only good thoughts. Instead, we have to develop self-knowledge about our emotions and mind just as they are, and that mental development will ultimately lead to changes in our feelings and our physical states. There are no shortcuts from being lost to being found, and although we can get good guidance from many sources, it is, in the end, only we ourselves who can develop our own mind. Enduring spirituality cannot be imposed from without. It is an inside job.

Both Dante and Assagioli tell us that our personality and our spirituality cannot be separated, that our mental/emotional development and our spiritual development are aspects of a single activity. We have encountered many people who dabble spiritually and get nowhere. Unfortunately, at the first moment of crisis, their unrealized spirituality blows away like dust. One reason for this might be that they were never really committed to transformation in the first place. Another reason, however, might be that in their seeking they were attempting to deny their own experience and doubts while trying to conform to the dictates of a particular religious or spiritual system.

We will not make that mistake. We will follow the guidance of Dante and Assagioli. Let us go to hell together...for the sake of discovering paradise and a way of harmony.

CHAPTER TWO

The Problem And The Promise

Because you wish to learn these secret things,
I'll tell you why I have no fear...

---- Beatrice, speaking to Virgil at the edge of Hell

In the opening lines of *The Divine Comedy*, Dante introduces us to a character, the Pilgrim, who is the personification of our capacity to completely miss the point of our life.

Midway along the journey of our life,
I woke to find myself in a dark wood...

The Pilgrim's "dark wood" is a frightening place. Any one of us could probably think of dark wood in which we have found ourselves at some point during the journey of our own life. One contemporary form of that wood about which we often hear is the depression, anxiety or stress-related illness that afflicts so many people. But there are also many subtler forms of feeling lost in the darkness. For some of us, it is the inner darkness from which we look out at life without feeling part of it, or the darkness we see in the world that causes us to seethe with silent rage or surrender to distraction and indifference. We can also get lost in the darkness of pride and mental arrogance, belief in our own unworthiness, or a frustrating desire to control reality.

In our own experience, having worked intimately with hundreds of patients over a thirty-year career, we have found that the single most pervasive form of feeling lost is living with a nagging sense of unfulfilled promise. That feeling of lost opportunity, of the road not taken, of the cup half empty, of another kind of life we never got to know, of "if only I had..." operates just beneath the surface for many of us, generating a quiet frustration, disappointment, and often an embarrassing and therefore hidden jealousy of the lives of others.

Dante's Pilgrim symbolizes everyone who gets lost, for whatever reasons they get lost, and his journey from the dark wood to a life of purpose and peace can equally be everyone's story. The potentials that make this transformative journey possible are already present inside every one of us.

Once the feeling of being lost in our life really hits us, our understandable first instinct may well be to make a change in our life— get out of a relationship or into a new one; get out of our job and into a new kind of business; get out of the place we live and move to a new place. Doing any one of these things can be an initial reaction to the nagging sense that we are missing out on something, that time is passing us by and if we just made any change at all, our life as a whole would change for the better.

That was the pilgrim's first instinct, too. Looking up from the dark wood, he sees the possibility of escape to something better when he notices a "hilltop shawled in morning rays of light." He immediately tries to climb toward the light, but his way is blocked by three terrifying beasts. The beasts represent our own fear-based instincts, which are the real "beasts" that block our way and stop us from going forward. By bringing these beasts into the picture, Dante is teaching us something very important about our own journey: We want to get to the light of our own potentials, but we find out that our way is blocked.

This, then, is the basic human tension. We have potentials, and we have obstacles that prevent us from fulfilling those potentials. This problem is compounded by the fact that we are generally incapable of seeing our own "beasts," our own obstacles, and until we are able to do that we will be ruled by them. This is why we all need a guide to point out our obstacles and help us to overcome them.

"...Once the feeling of being lost in our life really hits us..."

Virgil and Other Spiritual Guides

When Dante's pilgrim is forced back down into the dark wood by the beasts, a guide appears to help him. His guide is Virgil, the Roman poet born in 70 BC whose work Dante much admired and whose life paralleled his in significant ways. At the time he was writing *The Divine Comedy*, Dante was in exile from Florence, where the local government had condemned him to death by fire if he ever returned. He had become a wanderer, a peripatetic teacher and advisor to wealthy families, and he was destined to live out his adult life without ever seeing Florence again. Virgil, too, had lived in exile, his poems often speaking of his journey through a hostile world, and so it is understandable that Dante would have identified with him and chosen him to be a trustworthy guide for the Pilgrim.

Back in the dark wood, the Pilgrim hopes that Virgil is there to rescue him. Instead, however, Virgil delivers shocking news. He tells the sobbing and terrified Pilgrim: "You must travel down another road, if you ever hope to leave this wilderness."

The news from Virgil gets worse: "Now let me tell you what … is best. I'll be your guide, and you will follow me, and I will lead you through a world of pain."

A world of pain? That was exactly what the pilgrim had been trying to escape. What Virgil knows, and the pilgrim does not yet, is that if we do not learn to recognize our own obstacles, we will continue to repeat the same patterns of suffering over and over again. Virgil will lead the Pilgrim to a place—objectified by Dante as hell—where those patterns are made horrifyingly manifest because he knows that the first thing the spiritual seeker must do is to recognize those patterns in himself. Recognizing our own patterns of suffering is the first step toward freeing ourselves from them.

Hearing Virgil's bad news frightens the Pilgrim even more, and so Virgil provides him with further information to help alleviate his fear. It is information that speaks to all of us about our own hidden potentials for living.

The Source of Courage is Within You

Virgil first explains that he has come to help the Pilgrim as the result of a visit and a request from a powerful feminine force called Beatrice. Beatrice's glowing love and shining eyes had demonstrated to Virgil that she was from an entirely different dimension of reality than the edge of hell where he exists, and, sensing that, he tells the Pilgrim, he felt compelled to honor her request.

When Virgil met Beatrice, he asked her why she was not afraid to come down to the edge of hell, and Beatrice responded: "Because you want to learn about secret things, I'll tell you why I have no fear."

Those "secret things" are the potent, positive forces present in all of us, the elements of our spirituality that can be sources of courage throughout our life's journey. In his poem, Dante personifies these potentials as Virgil, Beatrice, Lucie, and Mary, but he expected that his readers would understand them as aspects of their own deeper reality. The Pilgrim's journey is Dante's way of depicting the path to discovering and receiving the benefits of these potentials that are open to all of us.

Virgil, the pilgrim's first guide, represents our capacity to be rational and discerning. He is our ability to observe, to think, to decide. As you will see, this rational ability is exactly what the Pilgrim will need to get through hell alive, and you can equate it to what you need when you are gripped by fears and negativity. In such a state, any of us becomes mentally immobilized. (As we will see later, the core of hell turns out to be not a pit of fire but a block of solid ice in which dwellers are completely immobilized.) To overcome our immobility, we need rationality, our own or someone else's, to help us observe the situation that frightens us, think it through, and decide what to do.

Dante, however, makes it very clear that our rationality, our Virgil, is, by itself, insufficient for fulfilling our spiritual potential. It is, however, fortunately connected to another, higher organizing process— our inner wisdom.

Beatrice is the symbol of this inner wisdom—what we in our practice refer to as the wisdom mind. She has a higher knowledge of reality, a connection to the loving essence of the universe. She lives in a reality that is beyond the bounds of time, with a constant awareness of life's intention to create, and she "has no fear" because she knows about the potent spiritual resources that dwell within us all.

If, like so many of us, you have never been educated to recognize the existence of your wisdom mind, you may, at this point, have no idea how to go about accessing the kind of freedom from fear that Beatrice enjoys, and you might even doubt your own capacity to do so. We know, however, that your wisdom mind is there within you, and, as we travel Dante's path together, we will be providing you with specific methods for experiencing and developing your relationship with that part of yourself.

In Dante's own life, there really was a Beatrice, a childhood acquaintance with whom Dante fell in love when they were both only nine years old. Sadly, however, they did not go on to become lovers or even friends. As a teenager, Beatrice was given in an arranged marriage to a wealthy older man. She died in her early twenties, and her death was one of the great losses of Dante's life. She remained in his mind as an image of unconditional love that had the power to generate inner peace and a renewed sense of purpose whenever he thought of her. It is only natural, then, that he would make her the central figure in the Pilgrim's journey, representative of the most crucial discovery he makes along the way. We will meet Beatrice again at the top of the mountain of purgatory. She is the Pilgrim's guide into paradise.

Having described Beatrice to the Pilgrim, Virgil then reassures him all the more by telling him that there are two even greater forces supporting Beatrice: They are Lucie and Mary.

In Italian, *luce* means light, and, for Dante, Lucie is the symbol of our human capacity for illumination, for illuminating grace, for those experiences of higher consciousness through which we come to see much more deeply into reality and even to experience its most cohesive, bonding essence, which is love. Mary is the symbol of that vast love.

In Christianity, Mary is, of course, the mother of the son of God. She is a central figure of the Catholic tradition within which Dante was writing, personifying the creative, compassionate force in the universe. Beautiful and quietly powerful depictions of Mary exist in churches around the world. And even Christians who have left the church retain images of her deep in their psyches.

As a symbol of mothering, caring, brave, powerful love, she belongs to a worldwide ancient and continuous lineage of figures representing the divine feminine. She is honored in the Koran of Islam as mother of one of the Prophets (Jesus), and is symbolically identical to the Chinese Buddhist figure of Kuan Yin, the female Buddha of compassion, and to Shehinah, the feminine Hebrew noun for the nurturing aspect of God.

It is encouraging to know that this nurturing, creative, compassionate, and inspiriting force is so widely recognized. We all must find a way to remember and honor her in our perception of what is real, because, by whatever name we call her, we are sustained by the fact that she is present in us and in the universe. Knowing her benevolence is available allows us to accept the challenge of confronting our inner hell.

The Pilgrim, having learned for the first time that there are such powerful and benevolent forces in the world wanting him to find his way and achieve his life's purpose, finally has the courage to follow Virgil into hell. And he tells us:

As little flowers from the frosty night are closed and limp,
and when the sun shines down on them,
they rise to open on their stem,

.…

my wilted strength began to bloom within me,
and such warm courage flowed into my heart
that I spoke like a man set free.

The Beginning of a Journey: Nancy, a Contemporary Pilgrim,Takes her First Steps

Perhaps you will recognize some aspects of yourself in Nancy, a patient who was able to move from suffering to living with more courage and peace by using the same universally accessible techniques we will be teaching to you.

Nancy, a high-level financial executive in her late forties and the mother of a grown son, was in a daily struggle with debilitating anxiety. She would feel it rising up inside her for no apparent reason at almost any time—a terrible sense of dread and impending doom. It might come while she was working quietly at her desk, waiting on line to see a movie, or just lying down to go to sleep. And because she didn't know when or why it might occur, she felt as if she were at its mercy, as if it had taken over her life.

She had already been to see several medical doctors, who had ruled out the hormonal shifts of early menopause as the reason for her anxiety but had not yet found any other physical cause. She had been prescribed a variety of medications, each of which seemed to work for two or three weeks, but sooner or later the anxiety would reassert itself. All she wanted, she said, was to feel "normal" again, to have her old self returned to her, and nothing she had tried so far had been able to give her that.

At her first therapy meeting, as Nancy was describing her anxiety, she suddenly began to feel it again in the middle of her chest. She said she hated the feeling, and it depressed her to think that her life was being taken away from her by something that was beyond her control.

We asked her to close her eyes and focus on the feeling. Then, after a few moments, she was asked to convert the sensation into a picture in her imagination. What would her anxiety look like? She immediately saw a picture of a broken heart, a heart split in two, and we suggested that she ask the broken heart what it needed to heal, and that she be open to whatever response she saw or heard in her mind or felt in her body. Nancy reported that she saw children, flowers, sunshine, and then she said, "innocence."

Asked to contemplate what meaning the word innocence had for her, she immediately responded that she had lost all innocence about life, that she now saw life as brutal, and that her heart was broken for three reasons: She was aware of time passing and her own aging; she had bittersweet feelings about her son, who was living far from home; and she could no longer tolerate the greed, lying, and small-minded politics she encountered every day in her profession.

And then she added a fourth reason—her disappointment at what she herself had become as opposed to what she could have been. It's not that she had wanted to be anything in particular, such as a doctor, a lawyer, a writer, or a leader of some kind. It was rather that she had lived almost fifty years and had never really known what she wanted from life. Good things had happened to her, things for which she was grateful, but she always had the nagging feeling that there was something important she just was not getting to and that time was running out on some dream she could not even identify.

A Dantean View of Nancy's Dilemma

Dante's Pilgrim is lost, as is Nancy, "midway through the journey of our life," which is, in fact, where we all must begin any transformation—in the middle of our life exactly as it is. It is for that reason that the Pilgrim cannot simply escape his difficult situation by climbing the hill toward the light; he first has to follow his guide down "another road," the road to hell, so that he can discover the causes of his own suffering. Without going to hell and gaining the knowledge to be found there, the pilgrim would be fated to keep repeating his patterns of suffering and experiencing the same obstacles to reaching the "light."

Dante portrays hell as a vast exhibition hall full of people who have in different ways caused suffering for themselves and for others. Within the context of 14th-century Italian Catholic culture, those causes of suffering were called "sins"—intentions and behaviors that separate us from God. We do not speak of "sin" in contemporary language, but whatever its name, something was definitely preventing Nancy from living in harmony with herself and the world; something was causing her to live in the hell of unpredictable, disturbing anxiety. Our teacher, Roberto Assagioli recognized this when, in his notes, he compared the suffering of his patients to the suffering of those in Dante's hell.

The contemporary parallel to being guided through hell in order to discover the causes of suffering is the psychotherapeutic process in which patient and therapist together revisit the patient's childhood in an effort to find the causes of his or her present suffering. Most psychotherapy, because it holds no view of human spirituality, restricts the entire therapeutic journey to this persistent focus on hell. Jung, Assagioli, and the field of humanistic and transpersonal therapy, however, opened up the view of human nature to include the journey to the patient's creative and spiritual potentials. By doing that, they provided something that neither religion-hostile psychology nor psychology-hostile religion had previously offered—a therapy based on a wholistic view of our nature, a view that fully connects our darkness and our light. By doing this, they were following Dante's lead, seeing all of hell, purgatory, and paradise as one unified vision of our nature.

Nancy came to therapy already in hell, and she needed the same reassurance the Pilgrim required before he could tolerate his downward journey. She needed to know that there were potent, positive forces available to her, and that there were great benefits as well as great struggles in store for her. If you were told such good news, you might want to believe it, but there is nothing more convincing than direct experience. With that in mind, we guided Nancy through a relaxation exercise that led her to her wisdom mind, her Beatrice.

Nancy Meets her Wisdom Guide

Sometimes, too much anxiety can block our mind to such a crippling degree that we become incapable of taking a test, speaking in public, going to an interview, confronting the boss, dancing at a party, riding in an elevator, being in large crowds, traveling on airplanes, looking down from heights, or even getting to the point where we can imagine trying something new. It was certainly possible that Nancy's anxiety might have blocked her from relaxing enough to benefit from the exercise we are about to describe, but, in fact, her wisdom mind was easily available to her.

First, she was asked her to close her eyes and let the soft chair in which she was seated hold her comfortably. In order to focus her attention, she was then asked to move her attention first to her left eye and to notice its sensations, and then to her right eye. Finally, she was guided to bring her attention to the space between her eyebrows.

She was then asked to picture in her imagination a wisdom figure or wise being of any kind. She saw a figure she described as a Tibetan monk floating in the air over a deep valley, and she then noticed an image of herself pinned in fear against the wall of a narrow mountain ledge. It was suggested that she ask the wisdom figure about her fear and that she be open to whatever response she received. When she did that, the monk responded by gesturing for her to leave the ledge and come out to join him in midair. Her response, however, was to look down into the abyss of the deep valley and press herself even more desperately against the wall. The monk gestured again, but Nancy still did not move.

At that point she opened her eyes and asked in astonishment, "What the hell was that?"

In our years of working with people's imagination, we've come to understand that the images it presents to any particular person have meanings that are unique to that person, and that it would, therefore, be inappropriate for us to make assumptions about what someone else's personal images might mean. To find out more about the images she had seen, Nancy was asked to close her eyes again and recapture the image of the monk. Once she had done that, she was guided to use her creative mind to imagine *becoming* the monk, to let her consciousness slip into his and imagine what the world would look like if seen through his eyes.

She became silent and still, and then she said, "Oh, my God!" After a few moments, she said that she had experienced light blazing from her eyes and a tremendous joy flowing through her body. She then sat quietly for several minutes taking in what she had experienced before leaving the office with the assignment to write about it.

Wisdom Mind Practice
. . . .

We will tell you much more about the wisdom mind as we go on, but this is a good point for you to experiment with it for yourself. Wisdom Mind practice is simple and straightforward. You may like our practice just as we describe it, or you may modify it for yourself after some experience.

One step of the practice is to imagine "a wise being, a wisdom figure of any kind" who appears on a path. We utilize this image because it activates your imagination— the principal place for the wisdom mind to display its knowledge to you. As Beatrice will say to the Pilgrim, "I tried to reach you through dreams and other means..."

There are many wisdom figure images that can be used. A wise old man or a wise old woman is often a natural choice. Memory images of a grandfather or grandmother can also be very effective, providing that they represent wisdom for you. (It is a sad commentary that many times people cannot find a wisdom figure among their memories of people they actually knew.) People have also used a lotus, a rose, the sun, a room of light, an angel, an ancient tree, Christ, the Buddha, among almost countless others, as their wisdom figure. These images can also be used in combination. For example, some people begin with imagining the bud of a rose that gradually opens, and then a spiritual teacher appears inside it. Different wisdom figure images often emerge spontaneously to communicate different kinds of information. One of our students had been visualizing the image of an Eastern monk, when, during one of his wisdom mind practices, the monk threw himself into a fire and never came back. In the student's next practice, an old crone appeared as his image of wisdom.

Many of us do not have a visual imagination strong enough to be capable of seeing an inner image. Instead, we may hear inner words or feel a change of emotion or energy as we contact our wisdom mind. These are important distinctions, and, as you practice this technique, you will begin to learn the specific ways in which your wisdom mind information comes to you and affects you. In fact, after some practice, you may find that you will be able to notice the information from your wisdom mind at any time without any conscious effort at all.

The visualization of a wisdom figure is most useful when we need to know more about the direction of our life, its purpose, values, and meaning, and the choices we are making for ourselves. You can also ask your wisdom figure about deep doubts you might harbor about yourself, about your hopes, or about spiritual or theological matters. The range of questions can be so broad because the wisdom mind, focused on the purpose of living, sees all questions and choices as relevant to the proper use of your life energy.

You may want to try this practice first with a friend to guide you, or you could put the directions on audiotape and be guided by your own voice. It is important to go slowly and be patient.

The practice will seem simple, but the answers you receive might surprise you. They may be one-word answers or long, elaborate inner visions. They may challenge you to re-orient your thinking. The important thing is to return to the practice again and again and to keep a diary of your experiences. You will be gradually cultivating direct access to your wisdom mind.

One final point: For whom does this practice work best? The people who use it!

Steps to Wisdom Mind Practice

1. Relax your shoulders, follow you breath, and let your body be held by your chair.

2. Begin to reflect on something you are wondering about at this point in your life... perhaps something about a decision you are trying to make... or something about yourself you are trying to understand better... or something about which you need guidance ...

3. Try to identify the question you are asking yourself. What's the question that gets to the heart of the matter? It's okay if you don't get it exactly.

4. And now turn your attention to the middle of your chest... and now, your mouth... and now, the sensation of breath passing through your nostrils... and now move your awareness all the way up to your left eye... and now your right eye... and now the space between your eyebrows... and now the middle of your forehead...

5. Now begin moving inside, into your imagination, and imagine a road or path stretching out in front of you... one you know or one you create... get a sense of walking on this path...

6. And begin to imagine, in the distance, a wise being, a wisdom

figure, of any kind … any kind at all … coming toward you …

7. Ask your question … and be open to whatever happens … take as much time as you want …

8. When the inner experience fades, sit quietly and absorb its meaning for you. Later on, make some notes for yourself.

9. If you feel that a wisdom figure did become available to you, you can later experiment with re-imagining that figure, and then using the power of your creative imagination to let your consciousness slip into that figure and look out through his/her eyes.

. . . .

When you have experiences like Nancy's, it is more important to sit with them than to rush to give them words. You can trust that, later on, you will naturally feel the desire to give words to the experiences. In fact, your mind will seek ways to give meaning to them because it knows that something of fundamental importance has happened to you.

You will be learning much more about the meaning of such illuminative experiences in the chapters that follow. For now, suffice it to say that by imagining the monk, Nancy had made contact, perhaps for the first time in her life, with a higher aspect of herself, that aspect personified by Dante in the figure of Beatrice—the wisdom mind. Initially, she was too fearful to let go of the mountainside—her instinctive, self-protective behaviors—and embrace the freedom personified by the monk, but by allowing herself to imagine seeing the world through his eyes, she was able to feel the joy that could come from living with that kind of higher consciousness. Assagioli taught that such higher consciousness objectively exists in each of us, and he was very clear about its value: "It is one of the primary experiences of living."

Nancy had been given her first glimpse of what it would be like to see the world through the eyes of her higher consciousness. Soon she would need to become aware of the causes of her suffering so that she could liberate herself from their domination and get to benefit from connecting with her higher consciousness more and more often. To do that, her next step would have to be downward.

Learning to Witness

Hell will always be with us in the form of our fear-based instincts and the reactions and patterns we develop around them. Since each of us is different, the hellish patterns that hold the most power will also be different for each one of us. In the following chapter, we will guide you on a tour of hell so that you can learn to recognize which of those patterns is holding you down and causing you to suffer.

One of the principle teachings Virgil gives to the Pilgrim is that he must not involve himself in any of the patterns he will see in hell. Instead, he is simply to witness and recognize what he is seeing. Virgil will tell him this repeatedly: Witness the pattern, recognize it, and move on: "So that you may have a knowledge…that is complete, go and see their torment for yourself. But let your conversation there be brief…"

We will guide you into more understanding of the importance of this practice when we get to hell together. For now, let us look again at our own pilgrim, Nancy, and see what she discovered as she began to prepare to overcome her own hell.

Nancy returned to therapy the week following her visualization of the monk and reported that she had been feeling anxious on and off throughout the week. She had consulted another medical doctor and was now trying an herbal supplement that she hoped would be the answer to her problems. If you, too, have struggled with anxiety, you will know what Nancy was going through. You are afraid that you are going to lose your mind, that the anxiety will take over completely, that you will never be able to get out of it, and you would be willing to try anything, take any drug, if it had the power to alleviate those frightening feelings.

That day, Nancy really started trying to understand why she was struggling with so much anxiety. She realized that, despite living her entire life in New York City, traveling around the world, and taking many risks in business, she had always been aware of an underlying, low-level nervousness that was continually focused on whether she would get through the day in one piece and get home safely. She had always thought of her nervousness as being "just who I am," but now it had somehow grown into this monster of debilitating anxiety. In the week since her previous therapy session she had thought about her experience with the Tibetan monk—his signaling to her to bypass her fears and join him in free flight instead of clinging to the mountain. "If only I could do that," she now said wistfully.

In fact, she could and would learn to do that, and so can you. Anxiety, which is only one of the many faces of fear, is a sensation felt first in the body as perhaps a tightness in the chest, the rapid beating of the heart, shortness of breath. Your mind becomes instantly alert and disturbed by these sudden physical changes, and you then begin consciously to dread how great the disturbing sensations will become. The dread mounts, the mind freezes, and the waves of fear rippling throughout your body increase in intensity.

It is possible, however, when the mind first becomes alerted to the beginning sensations of anxiety, to use your consciousness in a different way. You can learn to use a part of your mind to witness the sensation of anxiety as a physical phenomenon, a passing bio-chemical reaction, without exaggerating the actual danger of the moment. If you are able to witness the feeling of rising anxiety without getting caught up in the dread of what is to come, the feeling often fades and passes away. This is exactly what Virgil tries to teach the Pilgrim in hell—the power of witnessing.

Witnessing is not an intellectual exercise in which you think away your anxiety: Anxiety, in fact, overrides the ability to think clearly at all. Instead, you accomplish this with the part of your mind that observes. It is a specific mind-function that is treasured and deliberately strengthened by many of the world's meditative traditions because of the benefits it provides. The observing part of your mind notices all your experiences, good and bad, but does not experience them itself; it remains a constant witness, a constant presence. You can go down in flames in a plane or enter into spiritual bliss and the observing part of your mind will be there, too, witnessing the horror or the joy, but without getting lost in the experience itself. This is another one of those ideas, like the wisdom level of the mind, that you need to experience directly in order to understand it properly. We will teach how to have this experience, as we taught Nancy.

We asked Nancy to close her eyes, relax, and let the chair hold her. Once she had done that, she was guided to bring her attention to her feet and notice the sensations there, and then to move her attention to her left leg, to her right leg, and so on throughout her body. (Below, we have provided you with the complete steps for this guided meditation. Its purpose was to strengthen Nancy's ability to witness her experience.) When we had finally guided her to the top of her head, she was then instructed to slowly move her attention downward, distributing it equally throughout her body. This was a way for her to practice witnessing her different body sensations. After a minute or so, Nancy was asked what she was experiencing.

She said that about half way through the exercise, she had begun to see colors, which eventually became a vast river of purple flowing from the middle of her forehead. After that, she said, she had not heard any more instructions, but, upon opening her eyes, she felt that the light in the office was softer, and experienced a deep sense of peace. The river of purple that she had seen is a common experience when the mind enters into a meditative state and is experiencing subtler, quieter, inner energy. The part of your mind that witnesses is always peaceful, and when you spend any length of time in your witnessing mode, as Nancy did, your mental peace naturally increases and your conflicted and distracted mental states are quieted. Practicing your ability to witness your body sensations easily translates, in time, into an ability to witness your emotions and moods and even your own patterns of thought.

Witnessing The Body

Witnessing the mind and body is a basic skill in all meditative traditions. It is referred to variously as mindfulness, self-observation, non-judging awareness, witness consciousness, and silence. In Western psychology it is referred to as strengthening the observing ego. It is a way of strengthening the observing part of your mind that can bring the following benefits:

- Physically, it calms your body

- Psychologically, it strengthens your ability to be aware

- Spiritually, it helps your normal mental patterns to quiet down and allows your awareness to notice the subtler higher mental states, such as the wisdom mind.

You can do this sitting or lying down, but if you do it in bed, the chances are good that you will fall asleep. If sleeping is a problem, you should definitely add this exercise to your nightly preparation for sleep. Read the instructions through, and then try the steps.

1. Bring awareness to your feet... Now begin to bring awareness to your left leg... Now begin to bring awareness to your right leg... Now begin to bring awareness to your genitals and pelvic area... Now bring awareness to the sensations of your stomach... And now to the middle of your chest... And now shift to the left a little and begin to meditate on your heart... And now begin to bring awareness from your heart to your throat... And now your mouth... And now your left eye... And now begin to shift awareness to your right eye... Did you notice the feeling of awareness leaving the left eye and entering the right eye? When we shift awareness, we can actually feel it. And now bring awareness to the space between your eyebrows and move awareness up to the middle of your forehead, meditating on the sensations at the middle of your forehead... And now begin to bring awareness to the top of your head, noticing the sensations up there.

2. And now, at your own pace, slowly begin to guide awareness downward from the top of your head, guiding it slowly, gently, distributing it throughout your entire self... take your time...

3. (Wait about two minutes) Now begin to notice how you are feeling right now... When you feel ready, open your eyes.

What was the witnessing exercise like for you? Did you notice if your breathing slowed down? Did you feel heavier, or lighter, or warmer? These would all be signs that you entered a deeply relaxed state.

Did your awareness at some point not notice anything at all, even though you were still awake and present? This is a sign that your mind quieted down significantly.

What was your perception of time? Often, people will comment that time had really slowed down for them. In some cases, the experience will actually have been one of timelessness, a very pleasant, freeing sensation. These changes in your perception of time indicate that for a while your mind was actually liberated from its usual busyness.

. . . .

As Nancy practiced her witnessing skills at home, she gradually became better able to move through her feelings of anxiety without allowing them to derail her. In addition, she began to use visualization of the monk as a form of meditation. She had simply shut her eyes, as she had done in the office, bring a picture of the monk to mind, and ask him a question, remaining open to whatever the answer might be. That visualization was her way of strengthening her relationship with her wisdom mind, which she now hoped would become a source of centering and of the peace that would allow her to release her fears. During one such visualization the monk took her on a flying-carpet-ride around the world. And, while this might seem like a simple fantasy, the experience had a profound effect on Nancy because it provided her with the experience of exactly that freedom from fear that had been missing all her life.

Digging Deeper, Flying Higher

Nancy didn't become a different person; she still remained Nancy and she still experienced anxiety, particularly when she was traveling on business and in meetings with her foreign colleagues. She could use her newfound witnessing skills to acknowledge and get through those anxious times, but she did not yet understand why, with so much professional experience and so many accomplishments to her credit, she still felt so anxious.

Asked whether she had experienced some unexpected loss in her professional or personal life that might have caused her to lose confidence in herself, she thought for a moment and quietly said, "My son." She then went on to explain that she and her husband had always enjoyed a warm and close relationship with their son and that she, herself, had taken great pride in having "a great kid" and being a good mother. Now, she said, "because I did such a good job," her son was confidently exploring his own life halfway around the world in Japan. She was worried that because he seemed to be so attracted to Asia, he might settle down and establish a family there, but she also knew that her only recourse was to lead her own life and give him her love. Still, she said, "The passing of time and the way everything changes is very depressing."

When Nancy had finished describing her feelings and fears and fell silent, we asked her to close her eyes and picture her son in her imagination. She was then guided to imagine a light, coming from any source, shining upon him. She said that in her mind the room where she pictured her son was filled with light, and that the light began to intensify in brilliance until she felt she could no longer tolerate it. Even though it was entirely in her imagination, she felt the impulse to actually raise her hand to shield her eyes. But, despite her fear of its brilliance, the overall experience was thrilling, joyful. When she opened her eyes, she looked puzzled.

Nancy had just had her first breakthrough, her first illuminative experience of the inner light. Dante, as we said earlier, uses Lucie as the symbol of our capacity for this kind of illumination. Nancy, however, was puzzled because she had absolutely no reference point, no way for her mind to understand the experience.

We told her about a fresco by Fra Angelico on the wall of a monk's cell in the Museo San Marco in Florence in which Jesus is radiating such tremendous light that one of his apostles in unable to bear it and is pictured putting his hand up to shield his eyes. Nancy looked around the therapy office after that and saw with new eyes the prints of the Buddha in meditation and of Mary in prayer with their haloes of light. She saw the picture of the dancing Sufi whirling into a space of golden light, and she understood for the first time that these were depictions of real people having real experiences of enlightenment, illumination, the inner light, and that she, too, was beginning to know the deeper reality they were expressing.

From the Darkness to the Light

We have used Nancy's story to illustrate the journey of a modern pilgrim along the path Dante mapped so vividly many centuries ago. Her life had been, by any measure of society, a success. She had enjoyed a happy marriage, had raised a son who, by her own admission, was doing "just fine" on his own, and she had achieved success in her professional life. And yet she lived every day plagued by fears she could not control. She was not sick, she was not addicted to drugs, alcohol, or violence, and yet she was living in a hellish state. She knew, "in the middle of her life," that she had to find new answers, and she was motivated by her suffering to explore new realms of experience. She became a spiritual seeker out of sheer necessity, and in the process of facing her hell, she began to experience the higher potentials hidden in her nature.

Nancy is still on her journey. In the following chapter you will begin yours as we guide you through hell so that you, too, can begin to discover the behaviors and patterns of thought that may be preventing you from having the experience of more.

CHAPTER THREE
Hell — The Sea Of Pain

Dante uses the Pilgrim's journey through hell to provide us with a series of teaching stories. Each story exemplifies, in brutal detail, a negative state of being and illustrates how that negative state causes suffering not only to the person who embodies it but also to those around him. The importance of our journey together into hell is, first, to see if you recognize yourself in any of these stories, and then, if you do, to allow you to make a choice about what you will do with your new self-knowledge. When we move from hell to purgatory, we will teach you a variety of time-tested, effective ways to liberate yourself from these negative states.

Dante is brutal in his teachings because he was enraged by the way he saw people harming themselves and each other. Writing in exile, with a death sentence hanging over his head, he had no reason to hold back, to make things nice, to be politically correct. He depicted the entire spectrum of negative states of being, from the mildest—living a life of indifference—to the most violent and corrupt, reserving the darkest stories for people who betray others. He named the names of contemporaries who caused suffering, and he showed us through his alter ego, the Pilgrim, that he, too, sometimes fell into these negative states. Dante's reason for providing these graphic depictions was not, however, simply to enflame, and certainly not to entertain; it was, rather, to teach us an important truth about life, which he described as *contrapasso*.

Contrapasso

Dante's hell does not conform to the traditional religious view of a place where a punishing God pays one back for the bad things one did in life. Instead, it is a psychologically-sophisticated depiction of the way a particular law of our nature actually works inside us. We ourselves learned this law from Assagioli, and then re-learned it in our Dante study. Now we want to teach it to you because it has been, and will continue to be influential throughout your life.

Dante's hell stories teach us the law of *contrapasso*, which is exactly the same concept as the Eastern law of karma, the Biblical "As you sow, so shall you reap," the scientific concept of cause and effect (every action causes a reaction), and the modern concept of "what goes around, comes around." To teach this law to his patients and students, Assagioli used the simple formula: "Energy follows thought." If, for example, you put your thoughts into the negative state of greed and envy, you will cause yourself to suffer from the craving, dissatisfied energy of living in that state. In the old religious view, you are told that you will be punished in the afterlife *for* being envious (for violating the commandment not to covet your neighbor's goods), but the truth is that you suffer right now *by* being envious: The craving of greed and envy itself "punishes" you. The law of *contrapasso*, therefore, puts you in the difficult but hopeful position of being responsible for the way you use your mind and where you focus your consciousness. In the following chapter we will teach you to how to cultivate your consciousness in a way that will provide you with more inner freedom and greater spirituality. What you need to understand right now, however, is that your mind can lead you either to the doorways of illumination or to the dead ends of hell.

Students of Fear

When the Pilgrim goes down to hell and begins to grasp the pervasiveness of suffering in the human world, he tells us that his mind feels "centered in a sea of pain." We ourselves know, among our friends and colleagues and patients, some people who are especially sensitive to this sea of pain and who cannot bear to think about the suffering that goes on in daily life. But even the rest of us, who have thicker skin, might be caught short each time we hear about yet another fraud or betrayal or act of violence, asking in bewilderment, "How can people be this way?" When it comes to human-caused suffering, there is nothing new under the sun. Very little has changed between Dante's time and our own time. The obvious question then becomes: Why haven't we, as human beings, changed? Why haven't we had the change of heart that would lead to a saner, safer world?

The answer is that we have failed through the centuries to learn how to deal with fear.

Since fear will always be with us, we need to become better students of it, learn more from it, and decide what to do about it. To reduce the pervasiveness of hell on earth, we must individually learn how to reduce our fears and the negative actions that are generated by them and increase the amount of peace with which we live our lives. Assagioli was very clear about this: When he was asked about his goal for the people who practiced his ideas and methods, he responded that he hoped his students would become "examples of realized peace."

There are many sub-forms of fear, but in reality all of our fears, however they manifest, spring from a single source – our awareness of the fact that we die. We are all temporary, and we are all in this situation together. There are no exceptions—no wealth, status, power, scientific breakthrough, or religion will save anyone from his or her essential vulnerability. Even if you achieve worldwide fame and convince yourself that everyone loves you, you and your fame will still pass away, as Dante says, "like a gust of wind."

Since our fears come from our awareness of our mortality, the implication would seem to be that our greatest fear is the fear of death itself. In fact, however, it is our innate love of life and the fear of its loss that are at the root of our fear. It is not death itself we fear; it is the loss of this life. The supreme irony, then, is that our shared human fear is rooted in love. The next obvious question then becomes: What can we do about it?

The Three Choices

Once you grasp the reality of your actual vulnerable situation, you have three choices. The first is to try to escape from reality, the second is to try to gain power over it, and the third is to study it in more depth by going on a spiritual journey. Every one of us, as human beings, has made each one of these choices at some time in our life. There is nothing wrong with that, either, unless we begin to rely exclusively on either escape or power as the answer to our fears, because neither escape nor power is capable of producing an enduring antidote to our basic fear. During his solitary confinement in that Roman jail, Assagioli went on a spiritual journey that led him to a freedom beyond fear. Later, he went on to emphasize the importance of cultivating spiritual consciousness in his model of mental health because he knew indisputably, through direct experience, that it was the *only* thing that could help us in even our most desperate situations.

Dante's *Inferno* describes for us in terrifying detail the many ways in which our efforts to escape reality and/or to gain power over it not only fail to bring us peace but also cause suffering to ourselves and others. As a brilliant poet and a wise student of human behavior, he makes it easy for us to see these patterns in others; the challenge, however, is to recognize them in ourselves. Remember that the reason the Pilgrim had to descend into hell in the first place was to learn to recognize those behaviors that were preventing him from achieving illumination.

The poet and philosopher Mevlana Rumi provides a graphic analogy to illustrate this kind of personal blindness. Rumi tells us that we are not revolted at all by our own infected skin abscess. We would even put our infected finger into a bowl of soup, lick that finger to taste the soup, and not feel the least bit squeamish about what we had done. If, however, we saw someone else doing exactly the same thing, we would be disgusted and never eat a drop of that soup.

Our negative states of being are just like infections. None of us is offended by our own, but we all feel judgmental when we see them in others. Since, however, we are all, at one time or another, offended by other people, it would be reasonable to assume that others are offended by us. If that is so, Rumi tells us, we must be ready to apologize for our own offenses and, at the same time, show compassion to others for theirs.

Approaching the Gates of Hell

Now, alerted to Rumi's astute observation, we will go down into hell together to witness all the failed attempts to escape reality and/or gain power over it that Dante saw in his world. The poet depicts a path descending through nine realms of negativity and suffering to the lowest realm—a frozen pit from which all suffering emanates.

As our spiritual travelers approach the entrance, they see a powerful inscription on the gates, "Abandon all hope, you who enter here," which makes it very clear that hell holds no hope, no answers. That hopelessness, however, turns out to be self-inflicted because it is based on the fact that the people in hell refuse to recognize or learn from their own negative behaviors and states of mind, and are, therefore, compelled to repeat them eternally.

When the Pilgrim sees the inscription, he feels scared and

unsure. Observing his distress, Virgil says, "Now here you must leave all distrust behind; let all your cowardice die on this spot." The Pilgrim then tells us, "Placing his hand on mine, smiling at me in such a way that I was reassured, he led me in, into those mysteries." We all need this—to remember that there are potent, positive forces in the nature of reality, symbolized by Dante as Virgil, Beatrice, Lucie, and Mary—that support life, give us strength, and provide a reason to keep going no matter what lies ahead.

Choice Number One: Escape From Reality

One way people try to overcome the fear generated by knowledge of their mortality is to do whatever they can to keep reality at bay. They might deny that they care about life at all or they might try to numb their feelings and subvert their fears by engaging in some kind of addictive behavior.

The Indifferent

As the Pilgrim and Virgil pass through the gates of hell, they see souls frantically following someone who is carrying a banner that says nothing. Hornets and wasps buzz around the souls' faces and sting them as they walk. Our spiritual travelers have entered the realm of the Indifferent. Virgil tells the Pilgrim:

This wretched state of being
is the fate of those sad souls who lived a life
but lived it with no blame and no praise...

The world will not record their having been there.

The Indifferent so feared being overwhelmed by the knowledge of their vulnerability that they protected themselves by refusing to be touched by life. Now they are constantly being "touched" by the stinging of hornets and wasps, indicating that it is, in the end, impossible to pass through life without feeling. Blood and tears run down their faces and drip onto their feet, where maggots swim in the accumulating pus.

Indifference as an escape from human vulnerability can manifest itself in several ways. You might rely on sarcasm and cynicism to blunt your sense of caring, or you might continually distract yourself in order to prevent the more difficult aspects of reality from entering your consciousness at all. You might be instantly judgmental of people who suffer so that you do not even have to consider doing anything or feeling anything for them. Indifference might also manifest itself as a chronic refusal to decide or a passive acquiescence with whatever other people want. You might experience a chronic lack of energy or frequent fatigue. In the extreme, these behaviors can result in a trancelike state of disconnection that is exactly their goal—oblivion. Beyond all else, indifference seeks oblivion as a way to escape from reality.

The indifferent do not willfully cause pain to others; they are too preoccupied with protecting themselves. And yet they do cause suffering simply as a consequence of their own lack of caring. If you treat life as meaningless, as something you just need to "get through" as blindly as possible, you are demeaning its preciousness and reducing it to a tedious, purposeless struggle.

We do not see indifferent people in our therapy practice— they would be too indifferent to come. But we do see many people who are suffering from the indifference of others, most often that of a parent. That parent may have been self-absorbed, unhappy, sullen, ill, or worse—but what he or she communicated to his child was indifference.

"… The Indifferent so feared being overwhelmed by their vulnerability that they protected themselves by refusing to be touched by life…"

The effect on the child is a lifelong yearning for acknowledgment that he or she matters. As children, our survival depends on being seen and inspiring our parents to take care of us. As we get older, that need to survive expands to become a search for validation, for confirmation of our worth, for recognition of every little thing that we do. A part of us remains, in effect, a child in an adult's body still waiting for a simple sign that we are not invisible, that we are cared for. In Assagioli's model, our social self is stuck in a permanent pattern of searching for approval.

The indifferent parent, of course, appears to not care about any of this. He remains in his shut-off world, living on the fringe of feeling, just trying to get through life and stay alive. These people are trying to live unaffected by life, and the commitment of parenthood depends on exactly the opposite: allowing your child into your heart and mind. The irony of indifference is that it ultimately causes us to doubt our own humanity and to fear that we are, deep down, cold and incapable of loving. The pattern of indifference is used to protect us from feeling, and then we are stuck with the *contrapasso*— we fear that we are not capable of feeling and that there is something essentially wrong with us. Our indifference, in the end, backfires by causing the very suffering it was intended to avoid.

Assagioli also recognized a related pattern, that of our own poor self-parenting, our indifference toward our spiritual self, which he called "repression of the sublime." But he was also quick to point out that something of fundamental importance awaits us once we liberate ourselves from that indifference: "When [we] finally give up, when [our] resistance runs out, [we] discover that, instead of a feared annihilation, [we] have a greater life available to us." Assagioli then goes on to describe the illuminations that come from lifting the spiritual repression: "[We] are at times flooded by light and joy. [We] can feel the powerful heartbeat of the supreme unity in all things and all beings."

Einstein also spoke of this repression: "A human being is part of the whole, called 'Universe'... but he experiences himself, his thoughts and feelings, as something separated from the rest..."

He went on say that this separation was "... a kind of optical delusion of... consciousness. This delusion is a kind of prison for us, restricting us to our personal desires..." Einstein challenged us to "free ourselves from this prison."

Does indifference sound familiar to you? Do you practice it yourself? Did someone practice it on you? If you recognize it in yourself, understand that it is not the whole truth of who you are. If you were truly indifferent, you would not be reading this book. Any of us can have feelings of indifference, and at times act out of indifference, but that is only a mental pattern of protection based on our shared human fear.

At this point, we suggest you stop for a moment and write down to what degree you recognize yourself in the Indifferent. Be cognizant of the fact that indifference itself may tell you not to bother writing anything down. Do it anyway. Our experience tells us that Dante and Assagioli are right: These patterns, while they may seem harmless enough, are serious obstacles to discovering the much more interesting and lively parts of your nature. Why live trying to be oblivious to life? When we get to the school of transformation on the mountain of purgatory, we will actively transform indifference and liberate the love that is trapped inside it.

The Addicted

The second form of escapist behavior we encounter in hell is addiction. In contemporary terms, addiction generally refers to the compulsive use of drugs (including legal prescriptive drugs) and/or alcohol, food, sex, relationships, shopping, pornography, and gambling, with the latest development being addiction to Internet pornography.

If the Indifferent are trying to feel nothing, the Addicted are trying to feel soothed. There are a wide variety of biological and emotional theories about why any of us would feel the compulsive need to be soothed, but the common theme in the story of all addictions is the willingness of the person addicted to sacrifice every other aspect of his or her life to the satisfaction of that need. When we worked in drug and alcohol rehabilitation centers, we saw many lives subsumed by the need for another drink, another drug, another bet. Families of the addicted would come to the center and beg to understand why the bank president with the gambling habit had forged those papers to steal money for gambling, or why the carpenter father of three had driven drunk and hit those people at the bus stop, or why the college student had stolen all of his grandmother's rent money to score drugs. If you go to an open meeting of Alcoholics Anonymous, you will hear countless variations on these "war" stories—stories of the days and years of addiction.

The answer to why anyone would ruin his or her life for the sake of addiction lies in that person's pre-addiction feelings. Life felt like "too much; " he did not feel he was good enough; she felt she did not belong; he felt uncomfortable in his own skin, and the need to escape from those feelings was palpable and compelling. Our first book was about recovery from addictions, and in our years of experience we have worked with many patients in recovery who are engaged in an ongoing struggle with those pre-addiction feelings of vulnerability. We believe that the way to relieve these feelings is not by suppressing them but by discovering our inner wisdom so that we will be able to live in peace with our human vulnerability.

In order to give us a graphic image for teaching purposes, Dante offers the *contrapasso* that results from the compulsive consumption of food, alcohol, and/or drugs—living in a river of excrement. In the circle of the Addicted, the Pilgrim and Virgil see souls living in a constant stinking wetness and slime of their own making. This realm of compulsive consuming is guarded by Cerebus, a three-headed slimy dog-like monster who is the very model of craving need. The monster howls incessantly, its body twitching, wanting only to consume more. Virgil obliges by throwing handfuls of slime into its three needy mouths, and the monster immediately starts devouring the slime. What is the metaphoric significance of all this waste and excrement? It is the waste of people's lives.

Some addictions are about as subtle as a huge truck coming down the road. You will certainly know if you can not stop drinking or drugging or overeating or staring at Internet pornography or gambling. But there are also subtler forms of addiction—addiction to self-defeating ways of thinking—that you may not recognize as causes of suffering for yourself. Among the quieter hell states, one of the most devastating is an addiction to worry. We have seen many patients who consider worry to be normal way of thinking, and who don't realize the toll it is taking on their mind and body. They may complain of headaches or stomach problems, but they do not associate their physical symptoms with their chronic worrying. In our experience, people can be addicted to worry because of the soothing it brings them. That may sound contradictory. How can worry feel *good*? Some people, however, see worry as reassuring —a kind of thorough planning for the future. Because they have worried about everything they can possibly think of, they feel well prepared, which is, for them, relaxing. They might also ascribe a kind of religious faith to worry: If they worry about everything bad that could possibly happen, then possibly nothing bad will occur. One of our patients, Linda, worried that breaking up with her boyfriend meant she would be alone for the rest of her life. She thought about how she would handle eating alone, how she would handle traveling alone, and where she would retire to as a single old woman. She visualized these scenes in great detail as a kind of reassuring preparation that soothed the vulnerability she felt. She was twenty-seven years old at the time.

The Pilgrim identifies very strongly with the need for soothing and feels sympathy for those trapped in these negative states of being. Virgil, however, does not involve himself in the Pilgrim's emotional reaction. Instead, he asks only, "What are you thinking of?" He wants the Pilgrim to witness this hell state of being and then move on. Virgil is an expert on hell, and he knows the skills that are required for moving through it and out of it: You witness the suffering, acknowledge it by name, decide not to engage in it, and move on. We referred to these skills when we discussed helping our patient Nancy to overcome her anxiety, and we will teach you how to use them in the following chapter.

As we continue through hell, however, it seems fair to ask whether Dante, or any of us, has the wisdom to judge what is right or wrong about behaviors such as indifference and addiction? The answer is, yes, we do. The process of judgment is made elegantly simple with one question: Does the behavior increase suffering for ourselves or others?

Greed

The Pilgrim and Virgil next come to the circle of the greedy. In our experience, greed can dominate the mind even more pervasively than addiction because it seductively seems to offer both escape from reality (by equating happiness with money) *and* power over it (by thinking it will protect us). Greed helps us to gain the possessions that win approval for our social self and it temporarily gives us a sense of security and placates the survival anxieties of our biological self, thereby meeting two of our three basic needs as defined by Assagioli. The problem, however, is that it absolutely defeats our third need—our spiritual need for purpose—because it subsumes all other purposes to its own: Greed can become our reason for getting up in the morning, our entire reason for living.

Dante depicts the circle of greed as souls eternally pushing huge boulders back and forth. In life the greedy were obsessed with possessions and materialism, and so now they are now burdened with them forever. But within the greedy group, Dante also makes a distinction between the avaricious and the miserly. The avaricious focus on accumulating possessions while the miserly put their energy into clinging to what they have so that no one else can have it. These two groups are, therefore, in perpetual conflict, one wanting, the other withholding, which Dante depicts as the constant clashing of their boulders against one another.

Our Pilgrim notes that there are more souls here than in either of the other two circles he has seen so far. Dante has his alter-ego make this remark because he believed that his home city of Florence was being destroyed by greed. That was in the Middle Ages, but nothing has changed. Why does a CEO with two hundred million dollars find it necessary to acquire more money at any cost? Will three hundred million dollars be enough? How many individuals, families, companies, cities, and countries, are being destroyed by greed right now?

Greed is dramatic when it occurs on an organizational level, but greed within families can be the ugliest scene of all. Frederick, a patient of ours, is a wealthy man who does not want to give money to his adult children. He wants to use his money to make more money. In addition, he does not think his children deserve his money. He even debates whether to leave the money to them after his death. He has made out his will and thrown it away many times. Now, while he is alive, he wants the money for himself. He thinks about all the ways he can invest it, and he mentally totals his net worth several times a day. If he has made more money, he considers it to be a good day. If he loses money on one of his investments, he considers it a bad day. After a bad day, he cannot sleep. He has drugs to help him sleep, but after a really bad day no amount of drugs will put him to sleep. He is so absorbed in his greed that he does not have time to notice the alienation of his grown children and their families. He rolls his boulder around with him, day and night.

Virgil describes greed as a monster:

> *Her appetite increases as she feeds,*
> *And after she has fed, her hunger gnaws*
> *at her more keenly than it did before.*

The Buddhists share a similar insight about greed. They describe it as the realm of the hungry ghosts. These greed-based beings have huge stomachs and small mouths. No matter how much they put into their little mouths, they can never fill their big bellies, and their hunger is never satisfied. Dante called it *contrapasso*, the Buddhists call it karma, but both are describing a state of being that punishes us by choosing it.

If only we had enough money, we believe, we would feel no more fear. This promise of "no more fear" compels us to give in to greed, to cheat one another, to ruin one another—even members of our own family—and to sell out companies, cities, and nations. More and more we hear about the vast stockpiles of money accumulated by corrupt leaders in business, politics, and religion. And those of us without such wealth daydream about what it would do for us if we had it. You can see that dream in all the hopeful faces of people on line to buy lottery tickets, already planning how they will spend their winnings and live a life of happiness.

For the person with some spiritual development and a greater sense of life's purpose, however, this extreme form of greed is avoidable. The desire for money and things does not have to become hell. Money can be enjoyed for what it is but not made into a false god of protection. By addressing our fears through the cultivation of wisdom, money can stay in proper balance to the rest of our life.

Greed—always wanting more or fearing the loss of what we have—has a twin emotion, which is envy, the coveting of what we do not have. Imagine, for example, that you meet a friend after many years apart, and you find out that she now has a lot more money than you do. You try to be happy for her, but you cannot help yourself—you are competitive and envious. You suddenly feel that you do not have enough money; you want more. Greed and envy can happen to any of us, and now you have dropped down into it. You pretend to be interested in your friend's stories about buying a new home and traveling to exotic places, but you are suffering through this meeting, secretly resenting her good fortune and embarrassed by your own life. Envy loves what others have and hates them for having it. Its natural extension is to wish bad things

"Greed – always wanting more or fearing the loss of what we have got…"

for others: envy makes us glad when we hear bad news about somebody else. The Germans have a word for it—*schadenfreude*—shameful joy.

If you are get caught up in greed and envy you can continue to be consumed by those feelings or you can consciously choose to move out them. The willingness to move out of them is a step on the path of liberation and illumination. To refuse is to guarantee that you will continue to live in an inner prison of your own making, cut off from your higher potentials.

Do you identify with greed as a pattern in your life? If so, can you measure its power over you? Does it trigger its twin emotion, envy? Does it make you suffer to see others with more money? Do you feel that you really deserve to have what they have, and that you would be glad to hear they had suffered a significant loss? We all have these feelings; your own identification with them, therefore, simply proves that you are human. Write down any thoughts you have about yourself in relation to greed and envy. When you get to the school of transformation on the mountain of purgatory, you will actively transform the greed and liberate the love that is trapped inside it. Always remember, these patterns are not who you are.

The Second Choice: Power Over Reality

Thus far, we have showed you that indifference, addiction, and greed are attempts to escape the reality of our shared human vulnerability: The goal of Indifference is to feel nothing; the goal of addiction to feel soothed; and the goal of greed is to feel invulnerable and secure. But now we are entering a different realm, one in which human behaviors turn to power as a way to reduce vulnerability.

As we travel further into hell, we will see the full spectrum of the ways we attempt to gain power, from the primitive use of rage to protect ourselves from feeling hurt to the intentional cruelty through which the truly evil seek god-like power over life and death. Understandably, you may have trouble identifying yourself with these behaviors since the vast majority of us never link our intelligence, our intention, or our actions to the goal of causing such suffering. We might *fantasize* about doing so, but our basic identification with life prevents us from harming another life.

Because you do not associate yourself with these emotions or behaviors, you may not immediately see the purpose for witnessing them. What makes these circles of hell relevant to you, however, is that their very existence is disturbing and discouraging. The amount of intentional cruelty in the human world is a great weight that pulls us all down. And so, if we do not face the facts of this cruelty as part of our spiritual journey we will be subject to a spirituality of no enduring strength or value. What we tell you in this book must hold up in the face of cruelty as much as it holds up in the light of illumination.

The Rageful

At the next circle downward, our spiritual travelers approach the swamp called Styx—the realm of the rageful. We describe the scene in some detail because of its absolute accuracy in illustrating the effects of rage.

The Pilgrim describes

> *muddy people moving in that marsh*
> *all naked, with their faces scarred by rage.*

They fought each other, not with hands alone,
but struck with head and chest and feet as well,
with teeth they tore each other limb from limb.

These are the overtly rageful, but Virgil tells the Pilgrim that beneath the mud there are those who manifest their rage in sullenness and resentment. They are submerged, just as their rage was submerged in life, and their relentless sighing brings bubbles to the surface.

The Pilgrim and Virgil make their way around the rageful souls and continue their journey farther down the channel of the dead swamp. They think they are moving away from the rageful, but suddenly another soul rises up and confronts them. This meeting demonstrates the compelling quality of rage: It has an energy that sucks us in. The Pilgrim, who was generally sympathetic to the souls in the realms of indifference, addiction, and greed, now becomes cruel as a result of lingering too long in the circle of rage. Even Virgil, the expert on witnessing and moving on, does not get out of this realm unaffected.

Seeing this soul rising up from the swamp, the Pilgrim calls out: "…who are you, in all your ugliness?"

The soul answers: "You see that I am one who weeps."

And the Pilgrim, unable to contain his own rage, yells back: "… May you weep and wail, stuck here in this place forever."

The soul grabs for their boat, but Virgil, now in a rage himself, pushes him away and congratulates the Pilgrim for being so angry. His praise is extravagant. He embraces the Pilgrim and kisses his face, telling him that such indignation should make his mother proud!

The Pilgrim, still caught up in rage, tells Virgil it would really, really delight him to see the soul dunked deep into the slime and muck just one more time. And Virgil assures him that his wish will come true because it is such a worthy request. As their boat pulls away, they see the soul being attacked by others in the swamp, and then watch him attack himself.

Dante's teaching is clear: Rage is contagious. In modern times, we have seen entire communities swept up in rage and riots. And despite its destructiveness, rage is also seductive. In this case it is beyond the power of even our cool, rational guide, Virgil, to resist.

Rage is a secondary emotion; it rises up to protect you after you have been hurt. You might be in a conference at work, and your supervisor seems to be ignoring what you are saying. You feel slighted, or even criticized, and you suddenly feel this rising of energy within you. It is your rage. It may boil over into a remark you make or a hostile shift in your body posture, or you may successfully suppress it from reaching expression. This struggle happens to all of us. It is normal. But some of us want the rage; we want to utilize its power. We want to get our way at work by intimidating others. We want others to know that if they slight us, they will feel our rage.

The same dynamic is true in some marriages. Most often men—but also some women—use their rage to get other family members' full attention. One patient even commented that her husband actually seemed to derive pleasure from going into a rage. He would appear to be lost in his own ecstatic world, his eyes would glaze over, his voice would boom, his remarks would be uncensored and cutting.

Suppressed rage, on the other hand, seethes below the surface, sullen and resentful, the kind of rage that causes people to give their spouse the "silent treatment" for days. That is the kind of rage we saw in Michael, a patient who came into therapy a few months after suffering a major heart attack. He was a fifty-five-year-old Vietnam War veteran who brought thirty years of seething resentment to his first therapy session.

He was angry at his boss, his ex-wife, the military, the government, the driver in the car next to him, the slowness of the deli clerk, and on and on: He raged at life.

During his war experience, Michael had endured months under fire. Dead and wounded comrades passed through his camp on a daily basis. He had experienced vulnerability and fear with every cell of his body, and when he came back to America, he just wanted to be left alone. He withdrew into silence and communicated only with other veterans whom he trusted because they had shared his experience.

Whenever we meet someone who is in so much despair and rage, we know that this is not the only truth of who he is. We know that *something* has sustained him and given him a reason to live despite the severity of his pain. The fact that Michael had come for help indicated that he was searching for some way to strengthen his purpose for living.

There is a specific imagery meditation we use to help many of our patients and students connect with the source of their purpose and meaning, and we felt it would be helpful to Michael. Try it for yourself and see what self-understanding comes to you.

A Time of Meaning

1. Make your body comfortable ... Let the chair hold you ...

2. Now follow your breathing ...

3. Now let your breathing breathe on its own and just witness it ...

4. Now let your awareness go into your mind ... and into your memory ... and let a time come to you when you felt wholeness and meaning in your life ... let the details begin to come to you ...

5. And now begin to realize what the essence of that time was…
   What was at the heart of it for you? Take your time…

   ....

Michael's "time of meaning" turned out to be when he was introduced to scuba diving by one of his Vietnam buddies. At first, they went diving in the waters off the Virgin Islands among crystal clear reefs filled with color and beauty, alive with shimmering schools of fish. They both hated it. Michael said that it did not feel safe there. He felt exposed. He felt the need to keep alert to any possible danger, and he was afraid that the beauty and peacefulness of those waters might lull him into complacency. It was also difficult for him to believe in the beauty because he had been so profoundly confronted with the cruelty of the world. Beauty felt like fantasy; cruelty was reality.

The silence of scuba diving, however, was comforting, so he and his friend looked for other dive sites. Someone told them about diving in search of shipwrecks in cold water, and that idea appealed to them. Their first dive was in the deep, dark waters off the coast of Massachusetts. Michael felt most alive in the moments when he could dive down, down, down, eventually into blackness. The only sound was the sound of his breathing. He knew he was alive because he could hear his breath. He was alert and totally focused on breathing as he penetrated into the darkness.

The end of the dive would be a slow climb upward into the increasing brightness of the sunlight-infused ocean. He described the thrill he felt at the end of these dives. They were "real" because they brought him into direct contact with the fragility of life. There were no false promises or illusions. Each time he went down, he did not know for certain if he would make it back. For him, that was the truth of life.

And then there was the ascent, the movement toward light that Michael looked forward to. In our meeting, he tearfully expressed the relief he felt each time he approached the surface of the water. The relief came from knowing that he still *wanted* to make it to the surface, to keep living despite his emotional wounds.

Michael's story highlights the vulnerability that underlies most human rage. If you go into a rage, or if you see someone in a rage, you are experiencing a very hurt person.

Do you identify with rage as a pattern in your life? Do you use it to gain power over feeling hurt? Do you feel it rising up in you even over things of no importance? If so, you are getting a signal from your body that you are frightened and that your biological self is controlling you. Rage is a wake-up call to gain self-knowledge about what is frightening and hurting you. Make some notes about your reactions to the subject of rage, and when we get to the school of transformation on the mountain of purgatory, we will actively transform that rage and liberate the love trapped inside it.

The Gates of Dis

As we continue downward past the swamp of Styx, we come to the gates of the walled city of Dis. Dis marks a turning point in our journey. We are about to confront the intentional cruelty that exists in our world.

Dante takes us to Dis to teach us that the very existence of intentional cruelty is a source of deep disturbance and discouragement in all of our lives, a great weight that pulls us all down and even makes us question humanity's chances for survival. The distinction he makes between intentional and unintentional cruelty is the same one we make in our legal system. The degree of punishment prescribed by our laws is in part dependent upon whether or not we *intended* to cause harm.

Unlike the majority of us who do not purposefully set out to make others suffer, the souls in Dis have no such compunctions. While they, as human beings, are instinctively identified with life, they take pleasure in identifying with the decay and death aspect of the cycle. By acting from that identification, they experience brief pleasurable surges of power. Like little gods, they become the dispensers of decay and death, and their insane attempts to feel power over life are the primary causes of massive suffering in the world. Yes, evil exists: It is the complete identification of a human being with decay and death.

As the Pilgrim and Virgil approach Dis, they see more than a thousand demons perched on the gates, enraged and screaming, demanding to know why the Pilgrim, a living man, dares to walk into their region. The Pilgrim wants to run away, but Virgil begins to approach the demons. Afraid to be left alone, the Pilgrim calls out to his guide for reassurance. At first Virgil still sounds confident and reassuring, but then, a moment later, the demons block his path, and the Pilgrim suddenly sees his guide become downcast and unsure. Knowing what cruelty resides in Dis, we can understand why even the great guide Virgil is frightened.

When Assagioli was arrested by the Fascist police in pre-World War II Italy, he sank into a fearful state accompanied by an "intense tightening in my solar plexus" and a sense of dark fate looming over him. But then he went deep inside his soul and told himself, "This is my moment of dignity." He remembered the promise he had made to himself at age twelve to "always be present to myself," which to him meant always listening to the voice of inner truth, and he became determined not to answer any of the police's questions. As a result, he was handcuffed and put in a cell. The handcuffs eliminated any uncertainty he might have had about what was going to happen to him, and he again experienced the inner fear and darkness. But then he felt like he "woke up," and a "quiet but firm sense of inner dignity arose and pervaded my consciousness."

Spiritual Strength

Facing cruelty always requires tremendous courage. Seeing Virgil momentarily lose his courage caused the Pilgrim to falter as well. Fortunately, however, an angel appeared, reminding both travelers of the positive, loving forces that were supporting them and giving them the courage they needed to continue their journey into the revolting stench of the violent region of Dis. The angel is Dante's way of objectifying the entry into a higher level of consciousness that allows our travelers to reconnect with the spiritual source of their strength—the same inner resource that sustained Assagioli during his persecution.

Dante's teaching, like Assagioli's, is very clear here. You must develop spiritual strength in order to confront the cruelty and evil in human nature. Without that strength, evil is too intimidating for us to be able to do anything about it. It is anti-life and overwhelming.

Having seen how frightened the Pilgrim and Virgil have become, it is something of a surprise to see that the first souls they meet inside the gates of Dis are not obviously violent at all. Instead, they meet the souls of "heretics" trapped in open, burning coffins.

The Mentally Violent

Heretics are traditionally defined as people who make statements against a prevailing religious dogma, and to this day there are theocracies (governments ruled by clergy) that hunt down and punish such people.

Dante's teaching story, however, takes a different view. He is very specific about why he places these souls in the violent region of Dis. *They commit violence with their minds.* They seek to feel powerful by discrediting and manipulating other people's sense of reality. We have seen many patients who have been harmed by the aggression of someone trying to control their mind by systematically denying or dismissing their perceptions of a given situation. This pattern of mind-control occurs in families when there is a secret, such as the father's drinking, a sibling's mental illness, the sexual molestation of a child or a relative's illegal activities. The other family members are required to protect these secrets. In such situations we are required to deny what we have seen and what we know; we are required to deny the validity of our own feelings. Other examples of this kind of mental violence might include the sadistic parent who tells his child that everything she thinks and does is stupid; the fundamentalist preacher who wins compliance by frightening his followers with a threatening vision of a punishing God; or the scientific nay-sayer who shows contempt for other people's religious beliefs.

Dante provides us with a tragic-comic image to show how disconnected from reality the mentally violent really are. A soul is standing up straight in his coffin, pontificating about the nature of life and his own significance, while completely oblivious of the fact that he himself is trapped in a burning coffin in hell. The aggressiveness of his blind arrogance is impressive. He speaks so authoritatively that the Pilgrim even begins to doubt his own reality. Virgil sees the Pilgrim struggling and asks him, "What troubles you?"

The Pilgrim says that, having listened to the heretics, his mind is filled with confusion. Virgil responds by advising him to "make sure your mind retains those words you heard pronounced against yourself" in order to learn how he was manipulated, and then, pointing upward with his finger, he reassures the Pilgrim that the day will come when he will connect with his own higher wisdom. When that happens, he will feel his own inner authority and know his life's purpose. He will no longer have his sense of self undermined by the violence of other people's mental arrogance.

Healing from this kind of violence is always the recovery of one's own truth, one's own reality, learning again to trust that one's gut instincts, common sense, and inner wisdom are one's best guides. Since we all come into the world with these potentials, the healing journey becomes our rediscovery of their existence and beginning to test the reliability of their guidance in the course of daily life. When we make our way out of hell and begin to climb the mountain of purgatory, we will practice some of Assagioli's methods for restoring that inner authority.

What we see in the realm of heresy is a good example of the timelessness of Dante's wisdom. At first sight, you consider the concept of heresy archaic and no longer relevant to your own life. But once you grasp Dante's psychological astuteness, it's easy to see that mental violence causes suffering by confusing and diminishing people's self-trust and innate loving spirit. When we guide you down to the realms of betrayal, you will see this destruction of self-trust in even more extreme forms.

While we see patterns of indifference, addiction, greed, and rage all the time in our patients, we see the negative states of those who reside in Dis much less often because they are so opposed to learning and change. As a practical matter, the person who is trapped in a state of aggressive mental arrogance will not see any reason to seek help or transformation. He already knows! – so what could he possibly have to learn from anyone else? For these people, maintaining a sense of personal power in a frightening world depends upon their always being right—and getting everyone else to agree with them. Unfortunately, it usually takes an extreme mental or emotional meltdown, a complete crisis such as a serious illness, to break through their arrogance and bring their essential vulnerability to the surface. The courage to experience a change of heart emerges through vulnerability.

The Presence of Evil

Farther down in Dis, patterns of thought and behavior become less and less capable of change. Are some people beyond transformation? Are they too far gone, unreachable, unchangeable? Ideally, no, but realistically, yes. When someone crosses over into an obsession with gaining and maintaining power through cruelty, he becomes incapable of remembering that other people are real and sees them only as objects of his manipulations. We have worked in psychiatric hospitals with such patients, who are sometimes labeled sociopaths—the kinds of people who, in extreme form, might become serial killers. When you look into such a person's eyes, nothing looks back at you—their eyes are dead.

Using Assagioli's modernization of Dante's map, we have explored the inner worlds of many people, ranging from the severely disturbed to the mildly worried to the actively healthy, and, invariably, we come upon some kind of an anti-life pattern, an inner voice that seems to be identified with destruction, sometimes directed at others and sometimes at oneself. Freud, and many others before and after him, have called this destructive voice the "death instinct." "Don't worry," we tell our patients, "everyone has these thoughts," but this doesn't reduce very much the inner disturbance that comes with fantasizing about other people's destruction or mentally destroying ourselves.

If you practice meditation for a few months or are in transpersonal psychotherapy, you may have experienced such thoughts. Hildegard of Bingen, one of the world's treasured mystics, wrote beautiful music designed to take us all into higher states of consciousness and, right in the middle of such transcendent moments, she injected a harsh bellowing voice—the voice of the "devil"—into the music to stop it and terrorize us. Her point was our point: anti-life is in life. Those who are unreachable are totally identified with this instinct. The rest of us need to understand that it exists in everyone's mind so that we can accept it as part of our nature without giving it any more power over us.

Acknowledging your own anti-life patterns is the first step to freeing yourself from them. The second step is a deep commitment to spiritual development. Why? Because it is only by the direct knowing of the unity of deeper reality that you can reconcile and live in balance with the darkness that resides in your nature and in the world.

As encouragement, we would like you to take a moment to consider this question: What happens when you introduce light into the darkness? The darkness disappears. And what happens when you introduce darkness into the light? The darkness disappears. The wise teachers of every culture on earth know that light survives darkness but darkness cannot survive the light.

Dis: The Realm of the Physically Violent

You are now entering the realm of souls who have committed physical violence against others. "You will see," Virgil tells the Pilgrim, "the river of blood that boils the souls of those who through their violence injured others." The physically violent caused others' blood to flow, and their *contrapasso* is to live in a river of boiling blood. They live in the exact condition they created by making cruel choices.

This realm is guarded by the Minotaur, a confused monster who bites his own flesh, crazed and frenzied with rage. Violent and proud, he is forced to live with inextinguishable ranting and raving.

In the face of all of this violence, the Pilgrim struggles to take in the incomprehensible pain these souls have caused as well as the pain in which they live. It is the same struggle we have and you have when we consider the incomprehensible slaughter in Bosnia, Rwanda, Iraq, Syria, Palestine, Israel, Oklahoma City, New York, and Washington— the struggle to understand how people can "do this" to each other.

Dante tries to answer this question by describing a meeting between the Pilgrim and three souls in Dis. They recognize the Pilgrim by his clothes to be a man from their own "perverted" city of Florence, which, in Dante's time, had been the scene of much violence. The Pilgrim's heart is filled with grief because he understands that the violence of their environment had contributed to the violent choices these souls felt they had to make. It is the same for children now growing up in violent places—what else will they know? In response to the Pilgrim's expression of sympathy, one of the Florentines says he hopes the Pilgrim stays connected to his own soul as a source of guidance: "May your soul remain to guide your body for the years to come."

That gentle wish gets to the very essence of what has happened to the souls in Dis and, by extension, to the essence of all human cruelty. These beings have lost all contact with their soul. They have lost all connection to a higher purpose in life. They live only in their biological self, focused entirely on their survival and their perceptions, real or imagined, of threats and danger.

It is amazing that we can ever forget our soul or become so alienated from our deeper self. As we descend to the region below Dis, we will find out why we sabotage ourselves that way, how we break the bond with life that is our birthright, how our natural love of life gets twisted, and we get lost. We will find a way to understand even the cruelest of human behavior. We are approaching the bottom of hell, and Dante considers this place far worse than anything we have seen so far.

Geryon, Guardian of the Realms of Betrayal

As the Pilgrim and Virgil approach a pit that leads farther down, they see a strange monster floating up out of the stench and murky darkness. It is Geryon. He has a huge honest face with a smile that brings relief to the Pilgrim—such a welcoming face in such a horrible place. Virgil, however, counsels the Pilgrim to step to the side of this smiling being to see the poisonous claws and tail of Geryon's body. The big smile hides the poison.

Geryon is the face of fraud, "the one who makes the whole world stink." For Dante, all forms of frauds are forms of betrayal: The honest face draws you in, stimulates your innate love, and then manipulates you. You are fooled and harmed because of your own loving, trusting nature. Fraud counts on your being a good person and uses that goodness against you.

We are all extraordinarily resilient: We live with the knowledge that we die, and in the course of our life we have to adjust to and get past many problems—but we never get past betrayal. You may forget the details of the betrayal, but you never get past the fact that trusting your loving nature turned out to be a dangerous mistake. Betrayal robs you of your natural emotional birthright to be in loving unity with life. Your actual status as a "created being" who is inseparably part of creation gets stripped from your awareness and is replaced by a fearful, isolated self. You might temporarily re-establish your feeling of unity by being alone in nature, but once you return to the world of people, the hurt takes over again and you once more lose that connection.

Virgil, however, is not afraid of Geryon. He climbs on the monster's back and tells the Pilgrim to join him, saying that they need him to carry them down to the next realm of hell. Trembling and speechless at the thought of going near those poisonous claws, the Pilgrim nevertheless obeys his guide. Virgil holds him tightly in his arms and orders the monster to fly downward toward the endless flames and wails and moans of souls in the lowest realms.

The Need to Witness

Virgil knows this final descent is necessary because, as we have said, for our spirituality to be truly resilient, it must be based on a complete knowledge of the worst life has to offer. And the Pilgrim, despite his intense fear, clings to his guide, the embodiment of his rational self, because he knows that his guide is connected to and protected by the even higher states of consciousness personified by Beatrice, Lucie, and Mary. And so, even as he descends, the Pilgrim is already looking up. His courage comes from feeling connected to a loving and impassioned spiritual vision and the desire for truth.

This is the courage of all those brave souls in our human family who feel the imperative to witness human cruelty in order to wake us up to the world of suffering—Holocaust survivors who write memoirs so that we will never forget as well as war photographers and reporters who willingly put themselves in harm's way so that we may know the truth. The access we now have to that kind of knowledge is exponentially greater than it has ever been in the course of human history, and, hopefully, it will motivate more of us to study how to liberate ourselves from the behaviors of hell. "Be the change you want to see in the world," in Gandhi's simple but beautiful words, is exactly right.

Meanwhile, as we continue downward, Dante provides us with an intricate exhibition of all of the forms of betrayal. We will highlight just two of them—seduction and graft—because their impact in own time and culture is profound. You may never act on these or other forms of betrayal, but you are stuck with the fact that they exist all around you and may be diminishing your capacity to trust that life is essentially good. It would be easy enough to become disgusted and world-weary, even bitterly cynical after so much exposure to the betrayals large and small of daily life, and you need to recognize the effect they may be having on you.

Seducers

Geryon, having carried our spiritual travelers down to the next realm of hell, immediately takes off into the dark, stinking air. The Pilgrim sees souls walking naked in two lines that are moving rapidly in opposite directions. Horned devils are driving them along, whipping their backs, at times so forcefully that they are lifted off their feet. This is the *contrapasso* for seducers, people who have coerced others to meet their own demands: Now they are driven to obey the cruel, relentless demands of the demons' whips.

Seduction is the most intimate form of betrayal, the most devastating and disturbing form of which is the seduction of a child by the pedophile who uses the little one's naturally loving and trusting nature against him. The child's confusion and shame are intensified by his memory of the pleasure he felt at being treated so "special" and make it all the more difficult for the victim to disclose what has happened. Often, the abuse is not revealed until adulthood, when the betrayed one starts to make the connection between the early betrayal and his distrust of relationships, sexual conflicts, addiction, and feelings of powerlessness. The victim's bond with life, his natural love, and therefore his link to his higher potential, has been broken and needs to be healed.

Even without being physically molested, however, children can be seduced to devastating effect. When one parent confides the intimate details of his feelings about the other parent, he is inappropriately seducing his child's sense of allegiance. The father who comments on his daughter's developing breasts, the mother who kisses her adolescent son firmly on the lips, or the teacher who singles out one girl for special attention, are crossing the line of appropriate behavior between adults and children and endangering the child's normal emotional development. These are all betrayals because they count on the child's natural loving and trusting nature to manipulate the child for our own needs.

Grafters

Grafters betray the public trust and carry out their corrupt deals behind closed doors. Dante offers as their *contrapasso* a life hidden in the dark, beneath the surface of a pool of boiling tar. Demons busily toss grafters into the pool and hold them beneath the surface by jabbing them with grappling hooks.

Dante writes of the many forms of graft that took place throughout the cities of his time. Medieval Italy was not a unified country but a collection of city states, each with its own government and powerful families who had mercenary armies at their disposal. To visit Tuscany today and drive down roads winding through vineyards and olive groves is a blissful pastoral experience. The remnant of a medieval tower or wall is just another romantic, picturesque element in the landscape. In fact, however, these were fortifications, protection against the brutal mercenary armies sent by the government or the wealthy family down the road to intimidate you, destroy you, and take over your land.

Dante's longing for honest leadership and his despair at the misuse of power are more relevant than ever today when the betrayals of corrupt leaders spread their poison far and wide. Corrupt leadership is not just a political event reported on the evening news; it sets back our human development.

Certainly, we all cope with the seemingly endless news reports of scandal and corruption by making clever remarks in order to display our worldliness and skepticism, but you may wish to conduct an experiment with yourself by thinking of the latest scandal and then noticing what fantasies it triggers in your imagination. You will see that the scandal both enrages and discourages you, and it may even make you feel a bit of a fool for being honest yourself.

All of us, more or less, put our faith in the trustworthiness of social institutions. Otherwise, we would be individually and communally immobilized. The stockbroker and the investor, the clergy person and the congregation, the doctor and the patient, the siblings in business together, the husband and the wife, the grocer and the customer, the teacher and the student, and an almost infinite variety of other relationships all depend upon trust. Betrayals of that trust break down society and make it unsafe for us all. This is not a theory. Every day we are made aware of communities and entire nations in which corruption and betrayal have resulted in poverty, violence, and public chaos on a vast scale. Dante places grafters in the lower realm because they break the social contract, the commonly-held understanding that our biological instincts for self-preservation must be modified sufficiently to render us safe to (and from) one another.

The Bottom of Hell

This is the realm of complex betrayal. The souls here have linked their intelligence with cruel intentions and active violence to create a combination of forces that, Dante says, none of us can overcome because our humanity collapses in the face of such perversion.

The lowest realm of Dante's hell is not a fiery pit. The souls down here are trapped in a world of ice and frozen immobility.

The Pilgrim sees two souls locked together in the ice, butting each other's heads with insane rage. A third soul, whose frozen ears have fallen off, tells him the other two are brothers who killed each other in a fight over their inheritance.

Our travelers then move deeper into the cold center of this evil region and see a thousand purple-faced souls in the ice. The Pilgrim tells us that, "By fate or chance or willfully perhaps, I do not know, but stepping among the heads, my foot kicked hard against one of those faces." In the realm of such cruelty, the Pilgrim cannot resist his own impulse toward cruelty. The soul screams at the Pilgrim, demanding to know why he is being kicked and afraid that the Pilgrim has come to take revenge on him. In life, this soul was a traitor who betrayed his countrymen.

The next scene provides us with one of Dante's most grotesque images: the Pilgrim sees two souls frozen together in a single hole, one of them chewing with great hunger on the brain of the other. Seeing the Pilgrim, the eater stops for a moment, and "lifting his mouth from his horrendous meal," wipes "his messy lips" on the remaining hair of the chewed up skull. The two souls were both betrayers of other people, and then they betrayed each other. Their horrific *contrapasso* is, literally, to stay eternally trapped in the destruction of the mind.

As our travelers move on they come upon souls whose tears

have crystallized in their eyes. One of them, a monk, asks the Pilgrim to break the crystals so that his eyes can move for a moment until the next tear freezes and locks them in place again. The Pilgrim promises to do so if the monk will first explain why he is there. But, after the monk confesses his acts of betrayal, the Pilgrim grimly tells us that, "I did not open them," and feels an exquisite pleasure at having betrayed the betrayer.

In this story, Dante is teaching us that our Pilgrim is being drawn into the cruelty that surrounds him and is enjoying the brief pleasurable surges of power that occur as a result of his own cruel acts. Like us, he is only a student of hell. He does not yet have the sustained ability to choose his own reactions. If he is around cruelty, it stimulates the cruelty in his own nature, and he acts on it. Dante is telling us that we need to cultivate a higher vision for our own life so that we are never sucked down into this level of hell. By making just one wrong choice on this level you can ruin your life.

We are now close to the core of hell. Our spiritual travelers can see Satan, "the king of the vast kingdom of all grief." His lower body is immobilized in ice, the entire negative weight of all hell bearing down on him. His wings flail wildly, causing the icy winds that keep this lowest realm forever frozen. He has three heads, and each of his mouths is grimly chewing on the head of a betrayer, whose legs dangle helplessly in the air. Two of the betrayers, Brutus and Cassius, participated in the assassination of Julius Caesar, and the third, Judas, in the assassination of one of the hopes of humanity, Jesus. Betrayal and the *contrapasso* of betrayal go on without end.

We have asked you to stare at the stark reality of intentional cruelty and betrayal in the world because they will always be a part of life. You can attempt to escape from this reality, and/or you can try to

"... Our Pilgrim is being drawn into the cruelty that surrounds him ..."

feel powerful and in control in the face of it. Your third choice is to see these behaviors for what they are—the frantic and futile attempts of human beings to transcend their human condition—and to understand, once again, that the alleviation of fear is already waiting for you in the seeds of spiritual knowledge you brought with you into this world.

Now, as we begin our ascent from hell, we will help you to begin reconnecting with that knowledge. We appreciate the trust you have shown by coming this far with us, and we know that your trust will be justified by the increased peace and joy you will ultimately find for yourself.

CHAPTER FOUR

Learning To Move Out Of Hell

Since hell is always going to be with us, we need to become skilled at responding to it. Specifically, we have to recognize when we have dropped down into it, and we have to know how to move up out of it. Virgil began to teach these skills to the Pilgrim when he advised him to *witness* and *identify* what he was seeing without responding to or becoming emotionally involved with hellish behaviors and patterns of thought. We ourselves learned these Witnessing and Naming skills from Assagioli; we use them to help our patients every day; and we will now teach you how to use them as well. They are the basic skills you will need to tap into the power and potential of your consciousness and continue your journey up to the mountain of transformation.

Taking Care of Your Consciousness

Your consciousness is the part of your brain/mind that notices all of your normal thoughts, feelings, impulses, and sensations. It is also the part of you that can get absorbed in hell or expand into the spiritual states of higher knowledge and higher feeling. Knowing how to care for your consciousness is, therefore, always a wise use of your time and effort, because the reward is that you will begin to experience new depths of peace, mental focus, and absolute joy. First, however, you need to understand its three most important qualities: awareness, energy, and the ability to move through time and space.

The First Quality of Consciousness: It is Aware

For most people, consciousness is synonymous with awareness. "I became conscious of that" means I became aware of that, I noticed it,

I saw it. When we direct consciousness toward an object or thought, we become more aware of it.

Consider this quality of consciousness in the context of the example we gave in the previous chapter about meeting an old friend and becoming envious of her affluence. First you become conscious of the envious reaction you are having toward your friend. Then you become *self*-conscious about your reaction. Your self-consciousness begins to influence your behavior. You cannot focus on what your friend is saying. You cannot enjoy the fact that she seems to be genuinely happy to see you again. You notice you are scanning her comments for some hint of something bad—a health scare, a broken relationship, the death of a relative: *something* about her life to make your envious self feel better. You are more and more aware of a pull inward, toward nagging, negative thoughts about yourself and your place in life. Your consciousness, focused on your envy, increases your awareness and experience of envy. On the mountain of purgatory, we will teach you how to transform moments like this into positive steps toward wisdom and illumination.

The Second Quality of Consciousness: It is Energetic

Consciousness is palpable energy. All the spiritual and healing traditions that study the life energy that flows through and animates us know this. This life energy is variously called chi (as in Tai Chi, Chi Kung, and acupuncture), ki (as in the Japanese martial arts such as Aikido), the holy spirit (in Christianity), and prana (in the Hindu and yogic traditions). In Western complementary medicine, it is now referred to as "subtle energy."

To better understand this energetic quality of consciousness, try the simple experiment that follows.

Consciousness as Energy

1. Let your body relax in your chair... close your eyes...

2. Now bring your awareness to the sensations of your left eye... stay there ten seconds...

3. Now shift your awareness to the sensations of your right eye... stay there ten seconds...

What happened when you brought awareness/consciousness to your left eye? There was a change. Perhaps it suddenly felt bigger, or heavier, or lighter. Moving your consciousness into it made it feel different.

Then you moved your awareness/consciousness to your right eye. Your left eye suddenly felt less, or smaller, or different in some way, and your right eye felt bigger, or more, or heavier.

All you did was move your consciousness from one eye to the other. Consciousness caused a change in your experience of your eyes. The same is true for a thought. Consciousness can change the quality of a thought. If you move your consciousness into it, you give the thought more energy. If you take consciousness out of it, the thought loses energy. You might have a stupid thought, a thought not worth having. We all have many of them. But if your consciousness enters into it, the thought gets energized, bigger, becomes more than it actually is worth. William's experience is a good example of how we can energize a thought, in this case a negative one.

William, a patient, was an actor who had won the leading role in an off-Broadway play. Because of some brief, passing moments of disapproval from the director at the beginning of the production, he came to believe that the director did not like him. In his imagination, William began to rehearse conversations with the director in which he told him how much he disrespected his directing. William imagined elaborating on the director's lack of training and on his insensitivity in dealing with the cast. The criticisms went on and on in his mind until he became lost in these elaborate, imagined conversations. The reality was that the director treated William well and the play was going well, but those "facts" did not prevent William from directing the flow of his consciousness into energizing his sense of hurt and desire for revenge. His consciousness was, in effect, trapped in his revenge fantasies and was slowly creating a hell state of sullen rage within him.

To liberate his consciousness, we first tried rationally to convince him logically that his thoughts were becoming trapped in hell and needed to move on. By doing that, we were taking on the role of Virgil, the rational guide. William, however, needed something more than rationality to get his consciousness unstuck, so we then taught him how to observe his revenge thoughts as they went on and on his mind (a witnessing method we will show you shortly). This allowed him to step back and gain some perspective on his thoughts. Observing them, he felt he would be able to decide whether to join up with them and keep them going or simply choose not to pay any more attention to them and move on. Eventually he was able to move on, just as Virgil was teaching the Pilgrim to do.

Consciousness is energy. Wherever you send it, you send energy.

The Third Quality of Consciousness: It Moves in Time and Space

We can appreciate that this may be the most difficult quality of consciousness to understand: Your consciousness extends beyond your physical body and brain. This is the quality most often associated with the continuation of consciousness after death, the belief that we have a soul, or some essential life energy, that leaves the body and continues to exist in another dimension of time and space.

Recent explorations into this quality of consciousness have led medical doctors and research scientists to investigate anecdotal reports of out-of-body experiences. Patients undergoing open-heart surgery have, for example, reported their consciousness going up to the ceiling and looking down on their own body, seeing the tops of the heads of the operating team. Sometimes they report traveling even farther. A very dramatic example of this phenomenon is reported by Dr. Larry Dossey in his book, *Recovering The Soul*. After surgery, a woman told the doctor and nurses in the recovery room that she had "traveled" throughout the hospital during the operation. Her experience included going up to a high floor in a closed-off section of the hospital and seeing an old shoe on a windowsill. Later, members of the staff went to that windowsill and found the shoe. What makes this story even more amazing is that the woman had been blind since birth.

Probably the best known and most widely reported of all out-of-body phenomena is the near-death experience. There has been an increased incidence in the reporting of such experiences because, on the one hand, advances in emergency medicine have resulted in more people being successfully resuscitated from clinical death and reporting what they have experienced. In addition, published accounts of these phenomena have freed even more people to talk about their own near-death experiences without fear of being labeled strange or crazy.

The classic description of the near-death experience begins with a traumatic event—heart failure, a car accident, surgery, or some other physical crisis. The person suddenly finds himself out of his body and moving at high speed toward a tunnel. He passes through the tunnel into brilliant light. The qualities of the light are very specific. It is so brilliant that you cannot see, and yet it does not hurt your eyes at all. In addition, the brilliant light seems to be a living, loving presence. The person passing into it feels enveloped by it, safe, and completely at peace. Dante describes this state of being as the "heaven of pure light... light full of love."

The near-death experience then takes one of two directions. Either deceased relatives or friends send the newcomer back to continue his life or the person having the near-death experience "sees" his life reviewed in a series of rapidly flashing images.

Whether through deceased relatives or life review, the person in near-death receives information about how much (or how little) love he or she contributed to the world. The purpose of this insight is to now return to life and be more loving in all of your relationships so that you increase the love in the world.

While most out-of-body experiences are reported by people who have been near death, they can also occur under very pleasant circumstances, such as during a state of deep meditation. Rebecca, one of our students, used to go to a meditation group that was held in a Zen garden. She always experienced her meditation as a very quiet and private time. On one occasion, however, she had the experience of being pulled upwards as if floating above the garden. From that vantage point she was able to view the garden and the other people in her meditation group from a completely new perspective. Then, as soon as she began to become consciously aware of the uniqueness of what was happening to her, she felt herself being pulled back down into her body. The after-effect of this experience was, she said, profoundly reassuring because she felt freed from the limitations of her physical body. She had started going to the meditation garden because she was dealing with the death of a dear friend, and the out-of-body experience opened her up to a deep connection not only with her friend but also with all the other people she had lost in her life. Fully back in her body, Rebecca felt united with the trees and flowers and was joyfully absorbed in the waves of a bird's song.

Whenever anyone experiences such an expansion of consciousness, the dual after-effect is always to feel more inner freedom from fear and to wonder how the experience could have occurred. Consciousness is the part of us that moves beyond our body, and discovering this mysterious quality of our consciousness tells us we have much more to learn about our own reality.

Cultivating Our Consciousness

Taken together, these three qualities—awareness, energy, and the ability to move in time and space—indicate that our consciousness is a living, active force in us. It is like a fertile field we must learn how to care for and cultivate in order to reap its potential bounty.

The cultivation of your consciousness, as we have said, requires that you learn two simple skills: witnessing and naming. Personally, we first practiced witnessing as part of our Buddhist meditation training. Later, when we studied Assagioli's work, we learned how to use it in order to experience the difference between our consciousness, which does the witnessing, and the mental activity that generates our reactions to what you have witnessed. This is exactly the same skill that Virgil taught the Pilgrim when he told him not to become emotionally engaged in the hellish states of the souls they met along their journey.

Dante was telling us very clearly that if you allow your consciousness to remain in hell—as our patient William had been doing—you will be trapped and suffer as a result. There is nothing more to be learned in hell than to become aware (or conscious) that you are in it, and then to choose to move on.

We have taught witnessing for many years to patients like William and Nancy, whom we met in Chapter Two, as an invaluable way to gain insight into and liberation from negative states of being. The effects of witnessing are subtle and build with repeated practice. After you have tried the skills we outline below, we will show how they help you to walk a spiritual path in the footsteps of Dante and Assagioli. We cannot emphasize strongly enough how much benefit you will derive from including their practice in your daily life.

Witnessing the Mind: Who Am I?

Read the instructions first, then try it.

1. Have a pen and paper next to you.

2. Close your eyes and ask yourself this question, "Who am I?"

3. Witness what comes into your mind. After several answers rise into your awareness, write them down.

4. Repeat the practice three times.

   Do not be concerned about what came into your mind. We all

get both mundane and bizarre responses to the simple question, "Who am I?"

After you have done this several times, you will notice that your responses to the question begin to come more slowly, and there may be a few moments when you are simply conscious but with no mental content. In time, you will become more familiar with this state of consciousness-without-content. As was Assagioli's intent when he created this practice, you will be able to experience yourself as a peaceful witness of experience.

Witnessing the Breath

This practice and the one that follows use the breath as the object of your attention. They are similar to the Witnessing the Body practice we taught Nancy in Chapter Two.

Read the instructions first, and then try it.

1. Make yourself comfortable in your chair and close your eyes.

2. Now begin to notice the middle of your chest. Do this for 15 seconds.

3. And now begin to notice your breathing…

4. And now begin to let your breathing do the breathing… allow your breath to be the way it wants to be…without any involvement on your part … don't involve yourself at all … just observe it … just become a student of your breath …

5. If you notice that you are drifting off from focusing on your breath, that's perfectly normal … just return to it …

6. Don't work at this exercise … do it easily… Easy does it …

When people first try this, they often notice how difficult it is to just slow down, focus, and pay attention to one thing—their breath. Then, they often discover that they are trying to regulate their breath rather than letting it regulate itself. Our breathing knows how to breathe, but we might find we are bringing a kind of willfulness to it, exaggerating it so that we can notice it. And so, while this technique may seem very simple, it requires that you completely assume the witness position and let go of trying to control your breath or anything at all. It is a wonderful way to relax if you are feeling anxious or worked up in any way, and it can be practiced any time, any place, which makes it a very practical tool to have with you wherever you go.

The third witnessing practice is Variation on Witnessing the Breath. This time, as you notice either you are in-breath or you are out-breath, you will say a single word silently in your mind. As you try this, experiment with saying the word with the in-breath and then, at other times, with the out-breath, to find out which one feels more comfortable for you.

Variation on Witnessing the Breath

Read the instructions first, and then try it.

1. Begin witnessing your breath.

2. When you notice your in-breath, or your out-breath, say "One" or "Yes" or "Peace" or some other simple, positive statement in your mind.

3. Each time you notice your in- or out-breath, repeat the statement in your mind.

Practicing this combination of following your breath and saying a simple, positive statement in your mind leads to profound and positive physical changes that have been documented by more than thirty years of medical research. Your rate of respiration is lowered to a degree ordinarily reached only after seven hours of sleep, and your brainwaves slow to a rate associated with deep rest in the body, lowered heart rate, and a lower concentration of blood lactate (associated with anxiety). Other benefits include improved breathing patterns for people with bronchial asthma, lowered blood pressure in people with hypertension, reduction in symptoms of angina (chest pain in heart patients), greater ease in falling asleep, reduced stuttering, lowered blood sugar levels in diabetic patients, reduced psoriasis, reduced salivary bacteria, and a reduction in the nervous system's reaction to norepinephrine (the brain chemistry associated with anxiety) as well as increased mental stability and memory during new learning.

All of these benefits are the result of what Dr. Herbert Benson termed the relaxation response—a quieting of our entire physiology that is similar to the benefit we receive from a night of deep, restful sleep.

. . . .

Discovering Subtler Levels of Experience

All of the witnessing practices described above cause your consciousness to be focused, and when your consciousness is focused, your body slows down. But we are interested in this basic formula for more than its physical benefits. Your increasing ability to witness your experience will also make you much more aware of what is happening inside you mentally and emotionally. You do not need much subtlety or conscious focus to notice you are in a state of rage. You need only the barest consciousness to see that you are obsessed by money or driven by greed. Gluttony and addiction are about as subtle as a hammer. But you do need a subtler level of awareness to notice persistent, low levels of dissatisfaction or feelings of longing.

You may, for example, realize that you are in a bad mood, but you may not have noticed that you have been walking around with your jaw clenched in anger, with worries of imagined disasters running through your mind, with hurt feelings eating away at you, or with daydreams of escaping from all responsibility, any of which, if they continue, will drag you down into an even darker mood. But if you take just three minutes to engage in a witnessing practice, you will suddenly become conscious of these subtle thoughts and feelings that have been lurking below the surface of your awareness, which will allow you the opportunity to choose what to do with them. You can then decide to focus on relaxing your angry jaw, reassuring yourself that your worries are no more than fantasies, gaining a better perspective on your hurt feeling, or saying "no" to your thoughts of escape. By making these choices, you are able to disrupt the continuation of the unproductive thoughts and feelings before they take you down into the negative states of hell. You intercept the descent of your consciousness and free it up to be more present in the moment, more at ease as you go about your day. Witnessing, in other words, provides you with a tool for exercising more choice about what you think and feel.

This is a skill for better living. Our experience tells us that the quality of your daily life is not necessarily dependent on what arrangements you have made for your outer existence but on how you treat yourself in your inner world. Let us consider this in more detail by examining a very specific negative state that we, personally, consider to be endemic in modern society—self-criticism.

The Subtler Hell of Self-Criticism

When we visited the realm of addiction in the previous chapter, we told you about one of the subtler hell states—the addiction to worry. Another, equally damaging hellish pattern is self-criticism, which is one of the main causes of the persistent, low-level of dissatisfaction that plagues so many lives. The inner voice of criticism may focus on your lack of intelligence, a physical flaw, your ethnicity, your status in life, the impression you make on others, the mistakes you have made, or some other area in which you believe you are just "not good enough," and it may spread its negative effect in you as shame and embarrassment, debilitating levels of shyness, the constant need to please others, feelings of incompetence and failure, or feelings of being unlovable. Because you experience this self-criticism in the intimacy and privacy of your own mind, you believe it is you talking to you, and, therefore, you listen carefully.

We explore this mental pattern in psychotherapy all the time, and we can assure you that the self-criticism is, in fact, *not* coming from you. You did not come into this world feeling bad about yourself—you learned it. Your negative self-comments reflect the opinions you have heard about yourself from others and stored in your subconscious. People in your family, church, or school—the sources and places of social conditioning—may have said these things to you when you were at a highly impressionable age, and now you walk around with their opinions forming the definition of who you are. Even more insidious, however, is the fact that these opinions may not actually have been directed at you in the first place. You may have heard them said about someone else and, because of your own desire to belong and your fear of disapproval, you may have grabbed onto them as worries about yourself. You may even have fallen victim to the negative effects of advertising so much of which is designed to make people feel insecure or bad about themselves.

In Assagioli's terms, you have *identified* with the criticism as a description of you; you have made it a part of your identity. Assagioli saw it as the task of psychotherapy to discover a method that would help people *disidentify* from the criticism, and his explorations led him to conclude that the meditation practices of witnessing were the best way to find freedom from false identification with criticism.

We have taught witnessing routinely and with repeated success to anyone who struggles with self-criticism. First, we experiment with the various witnessing practices we have described in this chapter to see which one the patient likes best. Then, once he becomes comfortable with the practice, we ask the patient to go into the witnessing mode and simply name what he is experiencing.

Naming is what Virgil was teaching when, in the realm of the heretics, he advised the Pilgrim to "make sure your mind retains those words you heard pronounced against yourself" so that he would not allow himself to be manipulated by them again. The practice of naming follows below. After you have tried it, we will explain in more detail how it begins to give you freedom from the quiet hell of self-criticism.

Naming

This practice is adapted both from Buddhist mindfulness meditation and from Assagioli's work. It is simply a practice for noting and naming your ongoing experience. Read the instructions first, then try to do it for five minutes at a time at various points throughout the day.

1. Make yourself comfortable in the chair and close your eyes.

2. Whatever you notice, give it a name. For example, you may first notice that your eyes feel tired. Say inside your mind, "I notice my eyes are tired." Then wait to see what you notice next. It may be the sound of a car. Say inside your mind, "I notice a car sound."

Using the phrase "I notice" is a device to help focus your consciousness. The key is to include everything that you notice. If, for example, you notice that you haven't noticed anything, say "I notice nothing." If you notice that you have drifted off into a trance and haven't been doing the practice, then name that, too, saying, "I notice I drifted off." The beauty of this practice is that it's impossible to do it wrong.

. . . .

Naming, as you have probably noticed, does not focus specifically on identifying your self-critical thoughts. That is because when you consciously try to notice a particular *thought*, it has a way of not appearing. It is as if the thought knows you are looking for it, and it will not show itself. The naming practice, therefore, proceeds with the free form of simply noticing and naming *whatever* comes into your conscious awareness. Since the self-criticism is an established mental pattern, it will, in time, show itself—often as a negative comment on your very inability to do the naming practice properly. Your inner voice will say something like, "You're not doing this right," or "Why can't you do this?" or "You can never do these kinds of things." Or, the negativity may manifest itself as a feeling rather than a voice. You might, for example, feel increasing embarrassment or even a sense of urgency because you are not getting anything worthwhile out of the practice.

When you do notice a negative inner comment or mood, you simply name it as you would any other experience. What does this simple act do? You have just chosen not to become engaged with a mental pattern that, typically, you would get involved with and listen to carefully. You have, for that moment, not identified with it as *you* or as important. You have not given it your mental energy; instead, you have acknowledged it and moved on. Again, this is exactly the guidance Virgil gave the Pilgrim in hell: Witness what is going on, name it, and move on. Engaging in hell patterns is futile. They do only one thing—take you down with them. They go nowhere but down every time. They are the most predictable events in your inner life. Engage with negative states of being, and you will start to feel lower and lower.

Freeing Your Consciousness for the Experience of More

What else is happening when you do not identify with negative inner comments? You are freeing your consciousness for the experience of better things, more creative thoughts, noticing subtler levels of your mind. This is the interaction between hell and heaven in Dante's journey and the basis for Assagioli's insights about taking responsibility for your consciousness. If you let it get dragged down, you have short-circuited the journey you could have gone on, if even for a moment in time, because your consciousness was rendered unavailable for something more, something better.

The more skilled you become at witnessing, the better able you will be to choose where to direct your consciousness, and you will have more choice about what to energize, what to engage with in your mind, and what to simply name and move past.

You are a Center of Consciousness

The second purpose of practicing these witnessing skills is to help you feel a greater identification with yourself as a center of consciousness, a place of peace in the middle of all of your thoughts, feelings, impulses, and urges. With practice, this peaceful strength will be with you throughout your daily life. You will be able to sit on a bus or in a business meeting and quietly, peacefully observe both your inner world and the world outside more deeply and more fully. You will be able to notice how you react in particular situations without energizing those reactions or acting upon them. You will be building a quietly powerful skill—the ability to return to your peaceful, observing center whenever you choose. This level of choice will, quite literally, change your daily experience of yourself in the world. It is one of those experiences words simply are inadequate to describe; you will know it best only through your own direct experience. For that reason, we want to add to your witnessing and naming skills a practice that will help to build your identification with yourself as a center of consciousness.

This practice is a wonderful way to ground yourself if you are nervous or upset and to increase your quiet inner strength. We ourselves practice it, if only for half a minute, at various times every day and always receive its benefits.

Centering and Naming

Read the instructions first, and then try it.

1. Make yourself comfortable in your chair and close your eyes.

2. Place the palm of one hand on your navel, and then place your other hand on top of the first. You are now sitting with your

hands on your belly. This is your center.

3. Notice the sensations of your hands on your belly... Whatever pulls you away from your center, notice it and name it... For example, you may notice a twitch in your eye or an image of yesterday...Whatever it is, just name it and then return to your center.

It's important that you not force yourself to stay focused on your hands. They are your center. If you are pulled away, patiently name what has pulled you away, and then return to your center... Do this easily...

....

Reaping the Benefits of Witnessing, Naming, and Centering

These techniques may seem simple, but once you begin to practice them, their benefits will begin to flow to you. We saw this occur most dramatically when we were treating June, a thirty-five-year-old woman with HIV-AIDS who had been referred to us by her doctor because she was experiencing episodes of extreme fear and bitterness. She had refused medication to control her emotions, rightly asserting that she was having extreme feelings because of her extreme situation, and she immediately told us that she did not want to learn any "mental tricks" or relaxation techniques or be hypnotized out of her fear and bitterness. Quite clearly, she knew she needed some new way to be with her feelings, but she didn't want to deny them or distract herself from them.

We first trained June to sit quietly and say out loud any experience she was having moment to moment. She said, "Impatience," several times, referring to her impatience with the technique, but then she began to name other experiences she was noticing. After she had done this twice for short periods of time, we asked her to place her hands, one on top of the other, on her belly, and bring her attention to the sensations of her hands. She was then told that if anything at all took her attention away from her belly, which was certain to happen, she should name what it was and then guide her attention back to her hands. June was taught to consider her belly her center but not force herself in any way to stay focused on it; instead, she was simply to return to her center whenever she wandered away, making sure to name whatever it was that had distracted her.

The *Centering* and *Naming* technique met June's needs because it didn't ask her to either ignore or deny what she was feeling, but, at the same time, it provided a way for her to work more skillfully with those feelings. Gradually she began to realize that while she was certainly dominated by waves of fear and bitterness, there were other experiences going on in and around those feelings. By witnessing and naming those other experiences—questioning, religious searching, self-compassion, practical thinking, remembering—she was eventually able to direct her consciousness away from the fear and bitterness and toward those other aspects of her reality. She was learning to come up out of hell.

Learning to Choose

There is a predictable and fascinating process that follows from the practice of *Centering* and *Naming*. You are focused on your center when suddenly a long fantasy about a new relationship (or anything else) takes place in your imagination. You name it "fantasy," and then you return to your center.

You next notice that you have the impulse to get up and make a phone call (or check your calendar, or some other equally innocuous urge.) You have no idea why this impulse came to you. You name it and then return to your center. You next notice that you are worrying about your future. When you notice that you have gotten lost in worry, you name the worry and then return to your center.

What you are beginning to tune into is your inner world of impulses, images, thoughts, urges, and sensations. You are becoming conscious of what goes on inside you all the time. You may experience a fantasy (a new relationship), then an urge (make a phone call), then a change of mood (worry), but, normally, you don't see the connection. You think these are random events. As you tune in more, however, the connections start to become obvious. A fantasy creates an urge that in turn changes your mood. You are becoming aware of your inner world of cause and effect, and that is the beginning of a spiritual realization.

The souls in Dante's hell were experiencing the *contrapasso*, the effects that were caused by their own thoughts and behavior. As you become more aware of the way cause and effect is ruling your own life, you will realize that this could go on endlessly in the same old way—or, you can choose to change it. You begin to understand that you alone are responsible for how you let your consciousness to be used, or abused, by the images and impulses of your inner world. You can allow it to stay in hell, or you can direct it toward moving in another direction.

You are not responsible for what is in your mind. Your inner world has been filled with stimuli and messages from countless sources, but you are responsible for how you work with those stimuli and messages, what you give your consciousness to, and when you decide to withdraw consciousness. When Assagioli was interviewed by *Psychology Today* editor Sam Keen, he spoke about this responsibility for the right use of our consciousness. Keen tells us that as he was listening he experienced the dawning of an amazing insight: "My God—Assagioli's making us responsible for our identity." Dante is equally forceful about making us understand that hell is within us and that we have no choice but to become responsible for how we choose to work with that part of our nature so that it does not endlessly work on us.

We can apply the principle of choice to one of the more difficult hell states, rage. Rage appears as a surge of energy that suddenly charges up the body before we even notice it. We feel the need to get rid of it, to take an immediate action, to do *something* without waiting another second in order to discharge it.

This instant need to discharge the excessive energy of rage is the moment of tragedy. This is the moment when incredibly cruel words come flying out of our mouth, when objects get broken, when we push our foot all the way down on the gas pedal of the car, when we go looking for our gun, when we go charging at someone. Remember the Minotaur in hell gone crazy with the fever of rage? We become him.

One of our patients, Paul, had a lifelong problem with rage. In public, he could usually suppress it enough so that it would discharge as sarcasm or a veiled threat expressed in his tone of voice. Privately, however, his rage was overwhelming his wife. She knew he had been abused as a child, but that did not make it any easier for her to cope with his outbursts. She had finally had enough, and she wanted a divorce.

Rage can sometimes be helpful. It is the extra energy that surges into us to give us strength in the face of danger. It is the adrenaline that pumps through our body when we go into a state of fight-or-flight. But when the source of "danger" is your five-foot-tall wife, and all she did was make a mildly critical comment about your being late for dinner, your rage is not helping you; it is beyond your control. You have become the Minotaur over a passing remark about dinner.

We taught Paul the witnessing and naming practices at the same time we helped him to appreciate the childhood roots of his rage. Understanding why we react as we do does not always change our behavior, but it does help to diminish the degree of confusion and shame we feel about our inability to control ourselves.

As Paul sat, eyes closed, naming his inner experiences, he began to enter into a series of images and memories. The first image was of his sister winning a piano contest and then being insulted by their father because of a mistake she had made. On that occasion, Paul's sister had run out of the house and was not found for hours. The second image was of Paul himself as a six-year-old riding endlessly up and down the sidewalk on his bicycle. He was exhausted but he kept pushing himself to ride so that he could stay out of the house as long as possible.

The "lonely boy on the bicycle" became Paul's metaphor throughout his therapy. Gradually, he began to become aware that whenever his wife criticized him, he felt an immediate and severe shock to his system, and then the rage would come. In the therapy office, he was asked to imagine his rage. He was able feel it right there in the therapy chair, and he used his newly-acquired witnessing skills to observe it for as long as it lasted. That afternoon, as he took on the attitude of witness to his rage, he began to liberate himself from it. His basic kindness and his sense of fairness, previously obscured by the rage, began to become available to him and expressed more and more.

We sometimes feel the same sudden change of energy when we have an addictive urge. The urge to get high comes on suddenly, stays a while, and then—apparently miraculously—it goes. We discover that if we witness the urge that we have been acting on and in the process destroying ourselves, it becomes no more compelling than a passing thought.

We discover in time that we are not our anger, not our addiction, not our worry, not our negative self-criticism, not our fears. Yes, we have them in us, but they are not all that defines us. Once we have mastered the skills we need to move out of hell, we can choose to direct our consciousness toward better things. Like Virgil and the Pilgrim, we can "once again see the stars," the higher possibilities that are waiting for us in our nature.

CHAPTER FIVE

Climbing The Mountain Of Transformation

Hell is the repetition of suffering and the refusal to learn. Having descended to its icy, immobilized depths, having learned to witness and to name what you saw there, it is now time to follow Dante's travelers to the mountain of purgatory, where transformation begins.

Dante's purgatory is depicted as an island dominated by a steep mountain. It is a curious mountain because the higher you climb, the easier it gets. Virgil explains it this way:

This mount is not like others:
at the start it is most difficult to climb,
but then, the more one climbs the easier it becomes;

and when the slope feels gentle to the point that climbing up
would be as effortless as floating down a river in a boat--
well then, you have arrived at the [path's] end...

Dante's mountain is a school of spiritual development whose practicality and effectiveness derive from the fact that, rather than seeking to suppress your personality, it teaches you how to use your personality as the basis for spiritual practice. It is based on the principle that your natural spirituality is weighed down by the fear-based hellish patterns in your nature and by the discouragement of seeing those patterns of suffering alive in the world around you. As we go up the mountain, we will teach you how to liberate yourself from those fear-based patterns, with the result that your natural spirituality and its benefits will re-emerge into your daily life. If you recall what Virgil told the Pilgrim before their descent into hell, you will remember that he is the messenger of Beatrice, Lucie, and Mary, who are Dante's representations of the higher potentials that live in all of us. When we reach the top of the mountain, we will be prepared to reconnect with them.

The work of spiritual development and transformation takes place on seven ascending terraces along the mountain path. In hell, we saw only the suffering or *contrapasso* caused by hellish patterns of behavior and thought. In purgatory, however, Dante also shows us how to transform those patterns and the rewards to be gained from the work of transformation. On each terrace a group of souls is practicing liberation from a specific pattern that causes suffering.

As you climb the mountain with us, we will provide you not only with the modern interpretation of those patterns but also with seven different time-tested, effective practices that we utilize, in various combinations, with our patients so that you will be able to do this transformational work for yourself. Assagioli thought of all these practices as "food" that can nourish us if we put the right ingredients into them. By experimenting with the different practices, you will find the ones that are best for you, and you can then apply them to your daily life. The general principle behind all of the practices is that *they help you to solve problems by energizing the answers in your mind and heart.*

Interestingly, Dante has arranged the terraces of purgatory according to their order of difficulty as perceived by him, with the most difficult patterns closest to the base of the mountain. They are, moving from the bottom to the top of the mountain, pride, envy, rage, indifference, greed, addiction, and lust. Their order of difficulty for you, however, may be different from Dante's. None of these patterns is innately better or worse than any other; they are only better or worse for you. *The point is for you to personalize the mountain for yourself.* What patterns do you identify with most, or least, as causes of suffering in your own life? By giving us the Pilgrim's reactions to each of these patterns,

Dante gives us the chance to compare them to our own. As we climb, the mountain of transformation can become a crucible for creating change in your life right now.

When you begin these practices of transformation, it is natural that you will encounter resistance. Old habits do not want you to do anything new. They are patterns you have energized with your consciousness, and they do not want that energy to be taken away. They will continue to compete with your new practices for your conscious attention, and your new ones will have to be nurtured over time so that their benefits begin to reveal themselves to you.

Beginning is the Hardest Part

At the base of the mountain, close to the shore, Virgil and the Pilgrim meet the guardian of purgatory, whom Dante depicts as Cato, the Greek philosopher who lived from 95 to 45 B.C. and whom Dante admired for his integrity and love of freedom. Freedom is what we all find through transformation, freedom from fear and from the hellish thoughts and behaviors that spring from it. In fact, Virgil introduces the Pilgrim to Cato with these words:

> *May it please you to welcome him—he goes*
> *in search of freedom, and how dear that is.*

Cato then instructs the newcomers to go to the shoreline and find a reed to tie around the Pilgrim's waist. The reed, which is yielding yet strong, is Dante's symbol for the humility with which we all need to begin transformative practice. We need to be humble enough to recognize how little we really know about spiritual reality. The reed in Dante's *Purgatorio*, furthermore, magically replaces itself the minute it is plucked, reminding us that creation is a ceaseless and ever-present force in the world.

Having donned the reed of humility, the Pilgrim is ready to take a second preparatory step, and Cato instructs Virgil to clean the Pilgrim's face. The Pilgrim describes the experience to us:

> *My master placed both of his widespread hands*
> *gently upon the tender grass, and I,*
> *who understood what his intention was,*
>
> *offered my tear-stained face to him, and he*
> *made my face clean, restoring its true color,*
> *once buried underneath the dirt of Hell.*

Virgil is cleansing the Pilgrim's perceptions, preparing him to see with a fresh vision.

And so, equipped with humility, his vision cleared, the Pilgrim is ready to begin his climb. But even setting foot on the mountain is still a formidable challenge because, from his position at the base, it is impossible for him to see the top. That is the challenge all of us face when we begin such work. We cannot see where we will end up, and it is an act of faith to begin a transformative process without knowing exactly what to expect. Fearing the unknown, it is all too easy for us to be distracted or to believe we can be happy with less than spiritual fulfillment.

The Pilgrim, contemplating the climb, is gladly distracted by the arrival of a new boatload of souls at the island shore. Among them, he sees a former friend from Florence, a musician named Casella. The Pilgrim asks Casella to sing for him, and as he begins, other souls also gather round, happy to postpone the start of their arduous ascent.

In the geography of The *Divine Comedy*, purgatory is the place most like our everyday world, and the shoreline of the island is where most of us live. We, like the Pilgrim and the other souls who gather around Casella, seek distraction from the more challenging realities of life. Modern culture promotes leisurely distraction as the optimal goal in life, and most of us buy into it. We, too, would prefer to lounge at the base of the mountain, passing our time by simply enjoying what we have already achieved. But doing that, Dante reminds us, is, in fact, "living that life which is really a race to death." Time is precious, not something to be "passed" in a state of mindless distraction, and, as soon as he hears the sound of Casella's voice, Cato rushes in to berate the Pilgrim and remind him of his true purpose.

What negligence to stand around like this!
Run to the mountain, shed that [deadness] which still
does not let God be manifest in you!

The Wake-Up Call

Cato's admonishment is a "wake up call" that gets the travelers' full attention, just as a serious illness, the death of a loved one, or some other life-changing event can get our attention and become the impetus for us to want deeper answers to the purpose of life. Cato is telling the Pilgrim, as Dante tells us, that we are born to climb the mountain and find out what's at the top. Dante's very vision of the next step in human advancement—Beatrice—waits for us there. We must choose to wake up and climb because that is the point of living.

But what if the call never comes? Dante uses the entire first third of his *Purgatorio* to describe the souls who continue to live in "ante-purgatory," slowly circling the base of the mountain without ever even

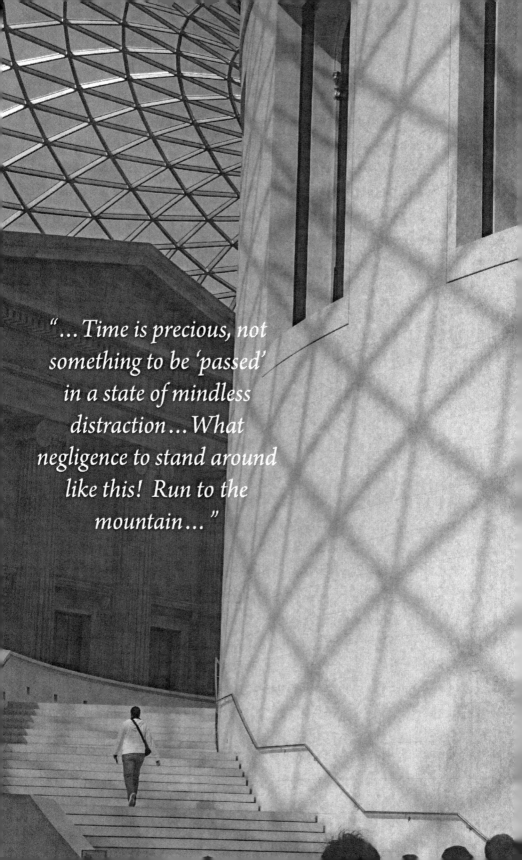

"…Time is precious, not something to be 'passed' in a state of mindless distraction…What negligence to stand around like this! Run to the mountain…"

realizing there is a gate that would lead them to so much more. Their wake-up call never came, or it came too late, or they were not listening when it did come, and now they have run out of time. They may wish for more spirituality in their lives, but they have not taken the initiative to do the work any student must do to acquire an education, spiritual or otherwise.

It is easy enough to pass up the opportunity for spiritual learning as we go about our busy lives, absorbed in fulfilling the demands of our biological and social selves. That is one of the reasons so many spiritual practices take place in deserts, in caves, on mountains, or in silent rooms—all places where it is possible to escape from the worldly demands that normally pull so relentlessly on our consciousness.

A Glimpse of Illumination

Awakened by Cato's cry, Virgil and the Pilgrim begin to climb the slope. They need to find the gate that stands at the entrance to the mountain path. After climbing all day, the exhausted Pilgrim lies down as the sun sets. Later that night, he has an extremely revealing dream:

> *... when our mind, straying [far] from the flesh,*
> *[not] tangled in the network of its thoughts,*
> *becomes somehow prophetic in its dreams,*
>
> *dreaming, I seemed to see hovering above,*
> *a golden-feathered eagle in the sky,*
> *with wings outspread and ready to swoop down ...*

The eagle circled for a while and then swooped down like a bolt of lightning, grabbing him and carrying him upward to a fiery sphere. The Pilgrim and the eagle both burn up in the fire.

The intensity of the heat in his dream awakens the Pilgrim. The sun has already been up for two hours, and he finds Virgil sitting next to him. Before the Pilgrim even has a chance to say anything, Virgil reassures him, telling him to not be afraid and to realize the real meaning of his dream.

The magical ability of Virgil to see into the Pilgrim's mind is Dante's way of teaching us that the higher levels of our mind—our rationality and our wisdom mind—can see the distorted impressions of reality created by our instinctual fears. This "magical" ability will be even more powerfully demonstrated when the Pilgrim comes under the guidance of Beatrice's divine wisdom. When you study your own wisdom mind as part of the journey of this book, you, too, will find that it sees right through your doubts and fears and tries to keep you on the path toward your goal.

Initially, the Pilgrim can only see the dream as frightening. He was, after all, flown into the sky by a bird of prey and burned up. Virgil, however, knows better. He knows the Pilgrim has had an illuminative experience that raised his consciousness so that he is now ready to pass through the gate to the mountain path. In fact, the travelers are now magically sitting very near the gate.

Virgil explains the Pilgrim's experience to him this way:

Before the break of day, while your soul slept
within your body... a lady came. She said, "I am [Lucie]
Come, let me take this man who lies asleep;
I wish to speed him on his journey up."

She took you in her arms at break of day
and brought you here. I followed after her.

Lucie represents our capacity for higher consciousness, for illumination. She is a symbol, in Dante's medieval culture, of the possibility for illuminating grace. Virgil tells the Pilgrim that Lucie has shown him the way to the mountain path.

What, in our contemporary language, do we have to describe the phenomenon of Lucie? Can you think of a contemporary explanation of your capacity for breakthrough experiences of expanded consciousness? As we lose the relevance of symbols such as Lucie, our contemporary minds have nothing to take her place, no way to understand such experiences.

Over the years, we have listened to hundreds of descriptions of experiences of consciousness expansion, including prophetic dreams, precognitions, synchronicity, inspirations, oneness, timelessness, harmony with all that is, out of body states, feelings of deep gratitude, tears of sheer joy, pervading bliss, healing and releasing shifts of energy, near-death journeys, entries into white light, cosmic humor and laughter, merging with beauty, boundless compassion, ecstasy, spontaneous physical healings of terminal illnesses, and scientific discoveries coming in visions.

Many times, however, people have no map, no guidelines for understanding their illuminative experiences. They refer to them as "weird," "strange," even "crazy," but they do not really mean those words, because, in truth, they were impressed by their experiences and wonder what they actually meant. They use dismissive terms because they are embarrassed to be claiming to have had an expansion of consciousness or "spiritual" experience. They guard against social disapproval by being the first to make fun of themselves.

Ideally, having a glimpse of illumination will be the impetus for us to do the work that allows us to recapture it and experience it again and again. For most people, however, the experience is so fleeting or so inexplicable that they either forget it or banish it from their consciousness. Learning to recapture that experience was the purpose for our teaching Michael, the Vietnam veteran, the *A Time of Meaning* exercise described in Chapter Three.

Patricia is student of ours whom we were also able to help recapture her time of meaning. She had attended a workshop in Arizona on Native American healing practices, including drumming, chanting, fasting, and spending time alone in the desert. Afterwards, having been moved by what she had learned and feeling a deep appreciation for the beauty of the land, she spent a few days exploring the area on her own. One morning she stopped her car to take a longer look at a particularly striking view. As she gazed at the desert, she began to feel a subtle wave of energy rise up from her solar plexus. She saw the sky glow with a rainbow of colors, "like the Northern Lights, only more vivid." The light was pervasive and she felt herself being lifted up into the colors and completely absorbed by them. After a period of time, which she described as feeling like both days and an instant, she found herself sobbing softly but feeling completely at peace. Later that day, however, she felt distanced from the experience, even unsettled by it, and she decided not to tell anyone about it. Instead of exploring it, she filed it away in the back of her mind.

It was not until many months later, having attended an imagery and consciousness class we were teaching, that Patricia remembered her desert experience and realized that she wanted to be able to understand

and appreciate it more fully. Remembering her time of meaning was the impetus for her to begin her spiritual journey.

Healing Our Wounds

When Virgil and the Pilgrim finally arrive at the gate that leads to the mountain path of learning, they see that it is guarded by an angel whose sword gives off a light so bright that the Pilgrim is partially blinded. At first the angel seems hostile to the Pilgrim, but when Virgil explains that they have been guided to this place by Lucie, the personification of spiritual illumination, the angel invites the Pilgrim to approach. When he does, the angel raises his sword and cuts seven scars into the skin of the Pilgrim's forehead. "Once entered here, be sure you cleanse away these wounds," the angel tells him.

Each scar represents a hellish pattern of thought, feeling, and behavior that the Pilgrim will learn to transform on the mountain terraces. Dante is teaching us that the path to the top—to higher consciousness—must include healing the scars we all have.

The Terrace of Pride

As Virgil and the Pilgrim pass through the gate and enter upon a narrow path, they pass through a cleft in the rocks and come upon the first terrace, a ledge with white marble carvings on its walls. This is the terrace of pride, and the carvings present us with images of the transformation of pride, which is humility. The first carving depicts the Annunciation, in which the angel Gabriel tells a humbled Mary that she has been chosen to give birth to Jesus. The significance for us of this religious image of humility is that we, too, must be willing to accept the fact that we have a role in God's Will, a role in the intention of the universe. In our modern culture of greed, power, and celebrity, God's Will may seem like a very remote idea, but it is an inescapable reality embedded in our very cells, and it is well worth making conscious contact with it. The second image is of King David dancing in humility before God; and the third is of the Roman Emperor Trajan halting his army to humbly listen to a poor woman's sorrow.

As the Pilgrim and Virgil gaze upon these images of humility, Dante offers us a sweet moment on the path. The Pilgrim comments that he is standing by the side of his gentle master, close to his master's heart. We are now traveling with a changed Pilgrim. He is no longer the frightened or enraged traveler we followed through hell. He is still vulnerable, but in a positive, open way. Having been through hell, he never wants to return, and he is both willing and eager to learn. Already he is more closely connected to the innate love that resides within him, and as he travels upward, an ever-expanding lightness of being will replace his heaviness of heart. Like the Pilgrim, each and every one of us can experience this sense of connectedness to the loving unity of all creation whenever our consciousness is liberated from the life-destroying patterns of hell.

The Little Self

Having first been presented with the transformation, the travelers now see the souls who are struggling with their pride. They are carrying huge boulders on their backs, so bent over that their faces are practically touching the ground. They are being humbled by the weight of their pride. Pride is love of the "little self," the part of our personality that believes its needs should be catered to, and the prideful are weighed down by their self-obsession, unable to see beyond themselves.

When we are prideful, self-absorbed, selfish, arrogant,

narcissistic, we may be totally oblivious of other people's needs, or we may be constantly devaluing others in order to make ourselves feel better. We might be briefly inclined to think well of someone who admires us, but very soon we will begin to devalue his admiration as well, because the narcissistic part of our nature demands that we believe we are better than everyone else.

Criticism is always the greatest blow to our pride. Whenever anyone disagrees with us, even on the most trivial of issues, we can feel threatened, and when that happens, our pride can spill over into rage, or, even worse, the need for revenge.

The prideful appear to be speaking, but because they are so bent over, the Pilgrim cannot hear what they are saying. He bends down and walks stooped over in order to listen to one of them. By presenting us with this image of the Pilgrim humbling himself to take the same position as the prideful sufferer, Dante is showing us that the Pilgrim identifies with and accepts his own pride. When Virgil sees this, he tells the Pilgrim to stand up. His burden of pride has been lifted, allowing him to stand tall while he remembers the humility he has learned. His inner progress is confirmed by the arrival of an angel with a face "shining like a trembling star at dawn." With a brush of his wing, the angel heals the first of the seven scars on the Pilgrim's forehead.

The healing produces an immediate benefit. As he begins to climb farther, up a flight of extremely steep steps, the Pilgrim realizes that the climbing seems easier than walking on level ground, and he asks Virgil, "What heavy thing has been removed from me?" His healing has begun.

Finding the Balance

At this point in the liberation process, it is important to make a distinction that Dante did not. When Dante advocates humility to negate the pattern of pride, he is speaking in absolutes—all pride is bad, all humility is good—and pride must, therefore, be extinguished. While such a black and white approach to good and evil would have been appropriate for the medieval poet, we take the more modern—and realistic—view that all human patterns of behavior are comprised of both positive and negative elements. In fact, the entire universe is made up of positive and negative elements in complex interaction and balance with one another.

Assagioli helps to make this distinction even clearer by reminding us that thoughts and feelings are living energetic forces in which positive and negative elements interact. Pride is negative when it leads us to become self-centered and narcissistic, but when it rises up to protect us or to motivate us to do our best or act with dignity, it is intelligent and positive. Humility, on the other hand, is positive—unless and until it prevents us from speaking up for and protecting ourselves.

We saw this negative become a positive when our patient, Gina, became involved in political manipulations at the company where she worked. A colleague in her department was trying to win a promotion by telling lies about Gina that reflected badly on her competence. When Gina heard about what her colleague had done, she went to her supervisor and stood up for herself by speaking directly about the lies she knew her colleague was telling and defending her own reputation for being a good worker. She protected her job and her salary by taking pride in her work. In that situation, her pride was a life-affirming, positive choice.

The goal, then, is not to eradicate pride and replace it with humility. When it leads to self-deprecation, the inability to defend oneself, becoming apologetic about one's very existence, excessive humility can be just as life threatening as excessive pride. Some situations, like Gina's, require acting with more pride and less humility; other situations might require the opposite. Finding that balance is like finding your center of gravity, the place where you feel at ease with yourself. When it comes to pride and humility, we like to think of that center as acting with dignity.

If pride is a pattern that is causing you suffering, here is an affirmation practice you can use to help find your balance.

New Affirmations

Using affirmations is a way to encourage new thinking, which will in turn awaken emotions that correspond to the new thoughts. The practice is part of the process of energizing the answer in order to solve a problem.

These affirmations are directed specifically at helping you to balance pride. You can use different words if these are not comfortable for you, and you can also use this model to create affirmations that will transform the other self-defeating patterns we will meet higher up the mountain.

When I am arguing, I will stop myself and take a deep breath.
I will listen better.
I will apologize more.
I am more interested in harmony than in being right.
I will stop devaluing other people in my mind.
There is so much to know; I will be open to learning.

I want to learn instead of pretending to know.
I can be all right without having all the answers.
I can relax because I am a child of God.
I have pride, but I am more than my pride.

You can practice your affirmation in a meditative style, sitting quietly and repeating it silently in your mind each time you feel your in-breath or out-breath. You can also choose an affirmation, say it to yourself, and then write about what it causes in you—what feelings, images, impulses, memories. Some of our students use affirmations randomly throughout the day as reminders of what they want to achieve in their self-development. And some are able to bring their affirmation to mind in the middle of an episode of excessive pride, helping the pride to recede and restoring their balance.

. . . .

Remember that this is only one of seven practices you will be learning to help transform your negative patterns. We will be teaching you a second one as we move from the terrace of pride to the terrace of envy.

The Terrace of Envy

As Virgil and the Pilgrim climb to the next level, they find themselves on a deserted path devoid of any sort of marker. They have traveled a mile by the Pilgrim's reckoning when they begin to hear the disembodied voices of spirits flying towards them. Once again their first contact is with the answer to suffering; the voices they hear are invoking generosity, the antidote to envy.

The generous are glad for the good fortune of others and

sympathetic to their suffering, while the envious want what others have and hate their good fortune for having it. Envy is poisonous, and, if that seems like too dramatic a statement, simply think about someone whom you believe to be in a better situation than yours and allow yourself to sink into envy. Immerse yourself in it and experience how truly ill and strange it makes you feel.

Dante's image of those who suffer the results of their envy is one of the most vivid of all the *contrapassi*. The envious spent so much time staring at what others had that now in purgatory they have gone blind. They crouch, sightless, against the mountainside afraid to move, crying for mercy and prayers. The Pilgrim is brought to tears by their plight and wants to reassure them that they will one day be able to see the divine light. He is actually practicing generosity by being charitable in the face of their suffering, and his second scar is being healed.

The Expansion of Envy

In the modern world, envy is exacerbated by our virtually unlimited technical access to information. We see the homes of the "rich and famous" on television, we hear news reports of others who have made vast sums of money, and all the while we compare their lives to our own. We may be happy as we are, but eventually our awareness of what others have begins to eat away at us. If we were not envious to begin with, having it "shoved down our throats," so to speak, every day, will eventually create envy. And then, once we are filled with the details of their' "fabulous" lives, the media pander to our envy by telling us about the crises and losses of those same celebrities—a divorce, an illness, the revelation of childhood abuse—all in order to give our envy the satisfaction of seeing those fabulous people suffer.

Because envy makes you want what others have, every time

"…The envious spent so
much time staring at what
others had that now…
they have gone blind. They
crouch sightless, against the
mountainside…"

someone else gets something more, it makes you feel that you have even less. We saw this happening to our patient Erica, a sculptor who envied her sister's success as a painter, fearing that every time her sister received some accolade or a positive review for her work, her own chances for success were being diminished. It was as if she imagined there were some finite amount of success to be had, and the more her sister got, the less there would be left for her. She could have used her envy positively, as the inspiration to achieve as much as her sister had. But, instead, she was focused on staring at and being eaten up by her sister's success. The phrase "sick with envy" precisely describes Erica's dilemma.

A Spiritual Perspective on Envy

Dante, however, suggests through Virgil that there is yet another way to transform envy—by looking at it from a spiritual perspective. From this perspective, he tells the Pilgrim, we are able to see that the more "good" others have, the more there will be for us as well. And, when the Pilgrim expresses his doubt that this is so, Virgil admonishes him:

> *Since you insist on limiting your mind*
> *to thoughts of worldly things alone,*
> *from the light you [get] only dark...*

> *The more souls...who are in love,*
> *the more there are [for us] worth loving;*
> *Love grows more, each soul a mirror mutually mirroring.*

He is reminding the Pilgrim that if we focus only on "worldly things," we will never truly find happiness, because fear of their loss oppresses us; our true source of happiness is always spiritual. And the more people there are who possess spiritual qualities, the more we will have them as well—both in the way others treat us and in what we can learn from them. When he meets Beatrice, Virgil tells the Pilgrim, he will be taught more about this very challenging principle.

The Pilgrim is learning, but he is still only on the second terrace of the mountain, and, like all of us, he is vulnerable to the pull of old habits and negative states of being. If you identify with the suffering of envy, create a series of affirmations that will help you to transform it. And add to that practice the one that follows here.

New Actions

It is obvious that changing our actions will change the quality of our life; the challenge is committing to and actually carrying out those actions. Assagioli saw that "the repetition of actions intensifies the urge to further reiteration and renders them easier and better, until they come to be performed unconsciously." Generosity generates an extraordinarily pleasing inner state and is well worth the time and effort it might take to energize it.

New Actions

Say something kind instead of complaining.
Give full attention. Listen well.
Express pleasure in someone else's good fortune.
Volunteer, donate your time, do public service.
As a reminder to yourself, sit down with a pencil and paper and make a list of

everything for which you can be grateful.

This list of behaviors certainly looks simple enough. Doing them, and remembering to do them often, is where you will find the obstacle. You can think of yourself as a scientist engaging in an experiment. Experiment with "say something kind" for two days and watch what happens to you. When you discover that you have forgotten to do it as many times as you actually did it, you will understand that new actions require the gathering of your will power to carry them out.

. . . .

After the Pilgrim has practiced generosity toward the blinded sufferers on the terrace of envy, he is struck by a light so bright that he has no way to shield his eyes from it. When he asks Virgil to explain its source, he is told that it is a messenger preparing him for the illumination that is to come, and that soon the light will not be difficult for him to look upon but will, rather, bring him much inner warmth and great joy.

The Terrace of Rage

As he and Virgil continue upward toward the third terrace, the Pilgrim notices that he is climbing effortlessly. He is truly experiencing the results of his healings—an increasing lightness of being. Approaching the terrace of rage, he falls into a trance and has an "ecstatic vision" of people practicing non-violence while others all around them are in a rage and clamoring for murder and revenge:

> *And then I saw a mob, raging with hate,*
> *stoning a boy to death, as all of them*
> *kept screaming to each other, "Kill him, kill!"*
>
> . . .

I saw him sinking slowly to his knees,
the weight of death forcing him to the earth;
but still his eyes were open gates to Heaven,

...

while he, in agony, prayed to his Lord
for the forgiveness of his murderers,
his face showing compassion for them all.

As the Pilgrim comes out of his trance, Virgil explains the purpose of his vision: "The things you saw were shown that you might learn to let your heart be flooded by the peace that flows eternally from that High [Fountain]." They have reached the terrace of rage with its love of power, and have been shown its answer, non-violence, a spiritual principle practiced around the world and personified by such great leaders as Mahatma Gandhi and Martin Luther King, to name just two of the best known. As a way to reduce suffering, the practice of non-violence has no equal; it transforms the violent instincts that lie just below the surface of our personality.

Rage, on the other hand, blinds you to anything beyond the violent thoughts that fill your mind. The terrace of rage is choked with a cloud of thick smoke "black as night." The Pilgrim is unable to see, but Virgil, his guide and reason, leads him through the pall, telling his charge to "Watch out. Be very careful not to lose me here." Remember that in hell both Virgil and the Pilgrim got caught in the realm of rage, and Virgil is well aware of its blinding power.

The kind of rage that rises up and blinds us to all reason is born of fear, and when we feel it taking over our mind or see it in others, it would be useful to ask ourselves what is frightening us. We had a patient, Bill, a smart, successful pediatrician, whose story illustrates just this kind of fear-based rage.

One evening Bill and his wife Ellen were to meet another couple at a restaurant for dinner. Ellen was taking a long time to get dressed, and Bill, waiting for her downstairs in the living room, was getting angrier and angrier as the minutes ticked by. Finally, his rage boiled over and he screamed up the stairs at her. Ellen had no idea why he was so angry; all she knew was that her husband had suddenly turned into a lunatic. When she finally came down, Bill gave her the silent treatment. Driving to the restaurant, he went through a stop sign, and when Ellen pointed out what he *had* done, he screamed that he had to do it because of her.

Needless to say, the entire evening was a disaster. Bill's sullen silence continued and as Ellen tried to draw him out, he just glared at her. The only saving grace was that the couple they were intending to meet had left a message at the restaurant saying they would not be able to make it.

Bill, meanwhile, felt completely alone in his rage, and his intelligence was working hard to find all the reasons it was justified.

In therapy, we helped Bill to step back and witness his rage. As he did that, he was finally able to see that he had always felt intimidated by the male of the couple they were supposed to meet for dinner, and he was afraid that the man would disapprove and criticize him if he and Ellen were late for their dinner date. The more he considered it, the better he understood that his rage had been driven by fear; he was beginning to move out of hell and learn about himself—he was beginning to climb the mountain of purgatory.

Reason Over Rage

Struggling in the dark, the Pilgrim then descends into more visions of destruction: "My mind became…so withdrawn into itself that the reality of things outside could not have entered there." His mind is trying to penetrate the truth. He is trying to find an answer to the violence in the world.

At this point, his vision is interrupted by a radiant light. An angel appears, brushing his wing against the Pilgrim's forehead, healing his third scar, and bringing the music of inner peace into his being. By going within himself and seeking the answer to rage through reason rather than allowing the rage all around him to draw him in, the Pilgrim had performed his own act of non-violence. The angel then shows our two travelers the way through the black smoke to the next terrace.

Before that happens, however, Dante takes a moment to introduce us to another kind of rage, the "righteous rage" that rises up within us when we see the world being destroyed by corrupt leadership. The Pilgrim was lucky enough to have an honest and reasonable leader in Virgil. But, Dante tells us, without proper guidance about how to benefit from "the nobler nature that creates our mind," we will imitate what we see in our leaders, whether they be the leaders of our government, our church, or our family. And if those leaders are immature, corrupt, and/or evil, they will not only affect the quality of immediate world or family events, they will also negatively impact the course of our human development by generating negative and false models of how to live. Once more we are being shown that there is a time when rage might be justified, and that it is how we direct our rage, how we respond to it, that gives it a positive or negative force.

If rage is a cause of your suffering, you might try to visualize a different way of behaving by doing the following practice, either alone or in conjunction with the others (New Affirmations and New Actions) we have taught you so far.

Visualization

Visualization taps into the power of imagination. Research has proven that our imagination links directly to our emotions and our body so that whatever we visualize, we feel. If you visualize something negative, you become anxious and your body becomes stressed. Your heart rate and breathing speed up and your blood pressure rises. When you visualize new positive patterns of behavior in your imagination, the newly visualized images gather energy in your mind and start to become a living reality in your way of thinking. Your visualizations become the basis for a new experience of yourself. Assagioli said that, "Images tend to awaken the emotions that correspond to them."

Visualize yourself behaving more peacefully in a variety of circumstances—at work, at home, and with strangers. Really see these scenes taking place in your imagination.

Remember that you are not striving for excessive peacefulness where you become passive and allow others to take advantage of you. Through visualizing various scenes, you will discover the kind of non-violence that is acceptable to you.

The Terrace of Indifference

It is almost midnight as Virgil and the Pilgrim climb to the next terrace, and the Pilgrim is extremely drowsy. He is, however, roused from his torpor by a crowd of people running zealously about, trying to make up for time they had previously lost while living lives of indifference.

Dante calls this level of the mountain the terrace of the slothful, but his interpretation of the word goes well beyond its common meaning, laziness. For him, to be slothful was to be indifferent to the pursuit of any purpose in life. Rather than responding to the challenges of life, the indifferent would prefer to avoid them. They give in to inertia and successfully cut themselves off from any feeling at all by feeling only numbness.

In modern terms, this might mean cutting yourself off from any kind of intimacy, which is what was happening to Jay, a patient of ours who found it too much trouble to invest himself in the emotional connection that is required to maintain a relationship. Each time he met someone new Jay would initially be happy, but quickly, as his new acquaintance required his attention or sought to deepen the relationship, he would pull back, become bored, and detach. It was simply too much trouble for him to sustain any real interest in anyone but himself.

When we asked him to imagine what it would be like to become involved with and care for another person, Jay immediately felt a worry rise up in him. His worry derived from the fear that caring was too risky because it would open him to painful feelings if anything went wrong. He did not actually remember ever having such painful feelings, but they nevertheless loomed as a great fear in his thinking.

The first step in his transformation was to bring his rational thinking, his Virgil, to the process of understanding his seemingly inexplicable fear. As we thought it through together, Jay realized he was afraid that the loss of someone he cared about might be too much for him and that he would break down or go crazy. In psychosynthesis, this is referred to as a polarity: Jay resorts to indifference because he is afraid of its exact polar opposite—being overwhelmed by emotion. By seeing these opposites in himself, he realized that there might be a middle way, a point of balance between these opposites. His goal then became defining that point. What would it look like, feel like? Jay's transformation began to move forward when he decided that "presence" was the balance point between indifference and being overwhelmed. For him, presence meant being attentive to others as well as himself. It didn't require becoming involved, but it did call for him to refuse to withdraw and detach.

As should be obvious by now, Dante was not a man of indifference, and because of that, his Pilgrim does not identify with the madly zealous souls he encounters on the terrace of indifference; their *contrapasso* is not his. As a result, his fourth wound is quickly healed and he and his guide pass on to the next level of the mountain. The climb is becoming easier.

Perhaps you can relate to the sense of disconnection that comes with indifference. If so, the following practice, as well as the others in this chapter, will help to transform your indifference into a more satisfying participation in your life.

Heart Meditation

The practice of cultivating presence, which we learned from Assagioli, is a psychological use of meditation. Its aim is to connect the person to his ongoing, living, feeling experience of himself, which then also enhances his capacity to be present to the living experience of others. This particular meditation utilizes a focus on the heart. It is both simple and profound and can also be used to help you transform any of the other patterns on the mountain of purgatory.

1. Place your hands on top of each other and rest them on your belly just below your navel.

2. Bring your awareness to the sensations of your hands—their contact with each other, the sensation of the slight rise and fall of your hands as your belly rises and falls with each breath … (Do this for a few moments.)

3. Each time you notice your mind being distracted by other sensations, sounds, or thoughts, just bring you awareness back to your hands... (Pause)

4. Now shift your awareness to your experience of the chair holding you... Notice all the points of contact between your body and the chair...

5. Now move your awareness to the center of your chest... Notice the sensations there—the slight movement of your chest with each breath... the sensation of breath passing down into your lungs...

6. Now move your awareness slightly to the left and become aware of your heart... Stay connected to your heart for a minute...

7. Now imagine yourself walking through your day with this connection to your heart...

After this meditation, write down what you imagined about your day as a result of staying connected to your heart. What was different? How were you different? What felt important?

In our experience, this meditation helps people to feel present, grounded, and more capable of being attentive to others. The focus on the heart is a way of directing your consciousness away from the mental patterns you usually rely on.

. . . .

The Terrace of Greed

Leaving the realm of indifference, the Pilgrim wanders in a dream state toward the terrace of greed. In his dream he sees a stuttering, cross-eyed woman with deformed hands and feet and a pale, sallow complexion. Still in the dream, as he gazes upon her, her stammer is cured, her hands and feet are healed, and "the color of love" suffuses her face. With that, she beguiles him by beginning to sing a seductive song. Virgil, however, again fulfilling his role as the Pilgrim's rational mind, appears in the dream and rips the woman's gown from her body, releasing a terrible stench that awakens the Pilgrim from his reverie.

The Pilgrim's dream symbolizes the attempt of the mind to imbue external things with the power to produce a happiness for us that they cannot produce. Greed gives this power to money and material things. Marcus, a patient in his 60s, discovered this truth when he came to therapy because he was feeling increasingly dissatisfied and impatient with everything in his life. He had never been in therapy before and could not believe that, at his age, he was, for the first time, asking someone else to help him feel better about his life. Nevertheless, he told us, things had gotten so bad that one evening, despite his skepticism about religion, he had actually gotten down on his knees and, in his desperation, asked God to help him feel happier. In response, he had heard an inner voice say a single word, "nurture."

He had instantly understood this to be a reference to his stepchildren, from whom he had always withheld his love. When we asked him why he had done that, he blurted out, "Because then they'll want some of my money."

Marcus was torn between two conflicting impulses—to hold on to his money as the hope for his happiness or to give away some of it as an act of nurturing and love. Buying another car, a bigger house, or taking more medication had not worked, and he had begun to realize that his skeptical prayers as well as his seeking therapy were both the results of a conclusion he had already come to—that he needed to transform something inside him.

Still contemplating his dream, the Pilgrim follows Virgil the rest of the way to the terrace of greed, where they come upon a group of sobbing souls stretched out face down on the dusty ground. These are the people who squandered their love on money and objects, who focused their consciousness on materialism, and who are now forced to stare at the barrenness of the material ground, incapable of looking up toward heaven.

Dante is once more being absolutist, presenting all greed and materialism as bad and only spiritual interests as good, when, in reality, we are, of course, both spiritual and material beings. If, however, we focus *entirely* on material things, if we allow ourselves to be consumed by greed, we will never be satisfied with life, because greed is, by its very nature, always hungry, insatiable. Each of us also has a basic, innate need to see beyond material things. If we do not look up, if we do not cultivate a larger view, a spiritual vision of living, our mind will be forever stuck with the severe limitations of materialism and an impossible job: trying not to notice that our material self is temporary.

One practice that can help you to refocus the energy of your consciousness when it is trapped by greed is to step back and *disidentify* from your behavior. This is a good way to remind yourself that you are not your greed. Your greed may always be with you, as a part of your personality, but it is not all of you, and certainly not the best of who you are.

Disidentification

One important precept in Assagioli's model of psychotherapy was to help his patients separate themselves and their identity from the thoughts and patterns of behavior that were self-defeating and preventing them from connecting with their innate spirituality. This is a practice he developed for that purpose.

1. Begin to connect with the thoughts that come over you in a greedy state of consciousness. Really allow yourself to sink deeply into them.

2. Now begin to connect with the feelings, the mood, that greed arouses in you.

3. Now stand up and connect with the physical posture that you go into when you are dominated by greed. Try to capture the expression on your face. Where do you hold tightness or tension in this state of mind? How does your voice sound?

4. Now literally take a step back and look at your greedy self. What do you see?

This simple process of first identifying with the pattern and then disidentifying from it gives us new insight into how we appear to ourselves and others in the state of greed. We may see a part of us we do not like, a part lost in obsession or insecure and afraid and, therefore, clinging to greed as a security blanket. Disidentifying works because we are more than our greed, and we are, therefore, capable of "stepping back" from it and looking at it more objectively. As we taught you in Chapter Four, there is a part of you—the observing part of your brain/mind—that can witness your internal experiences without getting lost in them. The witnessing practices in Chapter Four strengthen this important observing aspect of your nature. Disidentification relies upon the benefit of witnessing and simply adds the physical gesture of stepping back to dramatize the creation of distance from the pattern. If you like the practice of disidentification, you can apply it to any of the patterns you are trying to transform.

. . . .

Terrace of Addiction

Our travelers are now headed toward what Dante called the Terrace of Gluttony. By "gluttony," however, he means to signify much more than simply overeating; he means a compulsive need, a craving thirst, an irresistible love of consuming. We replace "gluttony" with the word "addiction" to put this broader definition into contemporary language.

Climbing upward, the Pilgrim realizes that he feels lighter than ever before. He is developing the lightness of being that will make experiences in paradise possible. His fifth scar has been healed, and he has only two left—the scars of addiction and lust.

Addiction and lust are physical desires or appetites, and so the healing angel Dante's travelers first meet on this terrace counsels them to turn the physical thirst in their nature into a spiritual thirst for a taste of God consciousness. Dante will have more to say about this thirst later in our journey when we get to paradise.

As they reach the terrace of addiction, Virgil and the Pilgrim are greeted by a beautiful sight, that of a tree heavy with fruit, giving off a sweet fragrance, standing right in the middle of the path. Water cascading down the mountain comes off a ledge and sprinkles the tree's upper leaves. It is a great relief for the travelers, who have seen so much misery on the mountain, to come upon this tree. But suddenly the terrace becomes a sadder place. The souls who live there come rushing by, dark-eyed, thin, pale, starving. They are the addictive who lived to consume. Now their *contrapasso* is to learn how to control themselves, to deny their urges to grab everything off the tree that is forever in front of them.

Dante and AA

The answer for the souls on this terrace is to find the correct focus for their hunger, for their thirst, for the desires and longing they feel. The addictive confuse their innate spiritual thirst with a physical thirst and respond to it by indulging in as much food, drugs, alcohol, shopping, and pornography as possible in the hope they will be satisfied. Their consumption, however, produces oblivion, not paradise.

Dante's fourteenth-century depiction of the distinction we need to make between spiritual thirst and addictive thirst has a 20th century parallel. The twelve steps of Alcoholics Anonymous (AA) are based on spiritual insights into the two basic elements of addiction—mental obsession and physical compulsion. The founders of AA realized that alcoholics have a kind of thirst that can never be filled by alcohol and created a process for achieving a new consciousness that was freed of physical thirst and focused on the fulfillment of spiritual thirst.

To reach this fulfillment, the twelve steps encourage a path of psychospiritual development that includes the following elements:

- Having faith and deriving courage from the fact that something in the world greater than our "little self" wants us to become whole and discover the truth.

- Realizing that the purpose of our life is to know that greater life's intention.

- Being willing to go down into our own darkness to discover the life-destroying patterns in our nature.

- Liberating our life from those life-destroying patterns through a conscious choosing of life-affirming attitudes and behaviors.

- Cultivating our consciousness to be capable of entering into direct contact with the deeper reality in the world that is our source of life.

- When appropriate, finding a way to transmit our learning to others.

There has been much debate about whether addictions are the result of character weakness, family influence, emotional conflict, or a genetically-based disease. Whatever the cause, however, the answer is that addicted people must learn how to live without the substance that is the object of their obsession. The transformational practice is to turn the destructive thirst or need into a spiritual thirst.

This is the very same practice that is being played out on the terrace of addiction. The addictive, protected and assisted by the angel of abstinence who nourishes them spiritually, are learning how to resist their urges.

Ultimately, addiction is a feeling of vulnerability that leads to a thought that leads to an action. To break down the pattern, we cannot change the feeling—that is our human nature. Rather, we must introduce new thoughts to take over from the old, addictive, life-destroying thoughts.

If you identify with the suffering of addiction in any form, the following practice involving the use of evocative words will help to strengthen your life-affirming thoughts and direct you toward spiritual nourishment.

Evocative Words

We all know that a word or two, positive or negative, can affect our entire day. Words have great power in our mind and body, and the evocative word practice is a way to make healthy use of that power.

The first step in using evocative words is to choose the word or words that best express the specific new quality you want to energize in your mind. Again, you are utilizing the transformational principle that you solve problems by energizing the answer.

AA, for example, uses short slogans such as "Easy Does It" or "Let Go and Let God" for this purpose. You can apply evocative words to any pattern of addiction or compulsion, with the goal of replacing needy addictive thinking with healthy peaceful thinking. One of our patients in recovery uses Dante's phrase, "In His Will is my peace," which he has shortened to "His Will," whenever he notices his old addictive patterns of thought starting up again. This is a way of evoking the awareness that peace will not come from addiction but from a life of purpose. Old habits remain in the mind, especially when we are under stress, long after the actual behavior has stopped, and evocative words help to create a new mental climate.

Once you have chosen your evocative word or words, write them on cards and spread them throughout your environment—on your desk, on your mirror, on the refrigerator door—so that you keep them frequently in mind.

Assagioli referred to this practice as creating a "beneficent obsession" to replace the destructive mental obsession of addiction. Taped on the wall in his private study, he had the words *Serenita* (serenity) and *Pazienza* (patience) staring back at him.

When you have decided on the evocative word or words you want to use, try this experiment on yourself:

1. Sit in a comfortable chair and let your muscles relax…let the chair hold you…let yourself sink into it…

2. Place the evocative word in your mind and focus on it as best you can…Do not be discouraged if other thoughts distract you— that's normal…just return to your word.

3. If ideas and images connected to the word come to you, watch them for a while and then return to the evocative word.

By doing this practice, you are "feeding" the evocative word or words into your mind, which will, in turn, generate new feelings in both your mind and your body. Whenever you have a minute, close your eyes and repeat the word silently several times in the privacy of your mind.

. . . .

The Terrace of Lust

The angel heals the Pilgrim's sixth scar with a soft breeze and shows our travelers the stairs to the seventh terrace. It is the terrace of lust, the last obstacle to be overcome before we reach the top of the mountain, where Beatrice waits to guide the Pilgrim and us into wisdom and illumination.

The geography of the terrace of lust is difficult to navigate; this is a very tricky place to be. The walls of the terrace have flames shooting out of them, forcing our travelers to walk along the edge of the cliff. The fear of being burned and the fear of falling require that they keep their minds very focused and their eyes directed straight ahead.

Dante has got it just right. This is exactly the action that one of our patients, Peter, had to take to liberate himself from a destructive pattern of lust. He had to walk past stores selling pornography; he had to not read advertisements for pornography on the Internet; and he had to stop staring at women's breasts as he walked down the street or rode the bus.

An important distinction needs to be made here. Dante was not denouncing sexual excitement in and of itself. Rather he was concerned with the suffering caused by the distorted, craving obsession with sex. He would have been an interested visitor to twenty-first-century American culture, which seems to be in a perpetual state of adolescent obsession with anything sexual. We Americans spend more money on pornography than on all other forms of entertainment combined, including books, movies, and sporting events. Many advertisements promise us that we will be more sexually attractive if we buy a particular product, even if it is a car, a bottle of soda, or a telephone. Direct and indirect sexual references in the media let women know they must improve their breast size, body shape, lips, chin, nose, eyes, cheekbones, as well as the texture and color of their hair in order to be more sexually appealing.

The sexual objectification of and selling to women is, moreover, now being directed toward men as well. There are more and more references in movies and media to penis size, penis functioning, baldness, and body shape. Men, in other words, are getting their equal chance to feel sexually and physically inadequate. High school athletic coaches report a growing self-consciousness and aversion among young men to communal locker room showers. There is an increase in eating disorders among men.

The answer for the souls on this terrace—as it is for the sex-obsessed in twenty-first- century America—is learning to treat one another with respect. As the souls pass each other, they are kind and dignified in their greetings. They are also transforming themselves by stating out loud the nature of their lust and announcing their new commitment to sex within a respectful relationship with a partner. The Medieval poet Dante is describing the two principles that govern the twenty-first-century understanding of how one recovers from sexual addiction—honest admission of the addiction and caring and respectful sexual relationships.

The Ring of Fire

Having witnessed the *contrapasso* of the souls on the terrace of lust, the Pilgrim himself must now face the flames. A ring of fire appears, blocking our travelers' path, and an angel tells them that they have no choice but to pass through it. The frightened Pilgrim immediately conjures up images of bodies he has seen burned, and, it is interesting to remember that Dante himself, at this point in his life, had been condemned to burning if he ever returned to Florence.

Virgil, however, reassures him, as he has done throughout their journey, that no harm will befall him:

> *Believe me when I say that if you spent*
> *a thousand years within the fire's heart,*
> *it would not singe a single hair of yours…*

The Pilgrim continues to stand staring at the ring of fire, immobilized and ashamed of his fear. Virgil then tries to motivate him by reminding him that Beatrice is on the other side of the fire, and with that reminder, he is suddenly able to plunge with Virgil into the flames.

At first the heat is overpowering, and the Pilgrim exclaims that jumping into "boiling glass" would feel like a relief. Thoughts of Beatrice, as well as his love and trust of Virgil, however, are enough to keep him moving forward, until he emerges unharmed as Virgil had promised.

This particular test vividly illustrates a consistent theme of the journey from hell to paradise, which is that love is greater than fear and gives us the courage to keep advancing toward a life that matters.

Prayer

Prayer is probably the oldest self-help technique on the planet. It asks us to enter into a quiet mental and physical state and then to direct our consciousness toward a struggle or hope in our life. Praying, we might be searching for the strength to handle a difficult challenge, or we might be asking for the liberation or release from some fear or behavior. The mystery of prayer is that there is, at times, some form of interaction between praying and subsequent events. This begs the question of whether the interaction is simply coincidence, or whether, in fact, the prayer did set something in motion.

What makes prayer different from the other practices we have shown you is that it presumes we are interacting with a higher power, a greater force in the universe than our little self, and that our prayer is drawing strength from that greater power. In terms of lust, we might pray for the removal of the obsession from our mind, or we might pray to look upon other people with respect, or to see other people not as objects of excitement but as children of God.

Because of the intimacy of prayer, we cannot suggest specific words for you to use. We can assure you, however, that prayer, like the other practices, does energize the answer in your mind and heart. It contributes to an inner climate of affirmation and the gradual liberation of your consciousness from patterns of suffering. Do not wait for some special time to practice prayer. You can pray for thirty seconds at various times throughout the day and begin to experience positive results.

· ·

Summarizing The Practices

We have now taught you seven practices using affirmations, new actions, visualization, meditation, disidentification, evocative words, and prayer. You can use any of them to transform any self-defeating pattern, and you can combine them to increase their effect. We use all of them in various combinations with our patients depending upon how each individual reacts to them. Do the same for yourself: Experiment with them to help you decide which ones you are most comfortable with, and which ones seem most helpful.

The Edge of the Forest

Having passed through the ring of fire the travelers come to a steep passageway that is wider than usual cut through the rock. The sun is setting behind them, and, now weary, they decide to sleep on the steps. The Pilgrim notes that the stars appear to be brighter. He does not know it yet, but he is falling asleep at the edge of a forest near the top of the mountain.

The Pilgrim awakens just before dawn. Virgil, who is already up, tells him: "That precious fruit which all men eagerly go searching for on many different trees will give, today, peace to your hungry soul." Virgil is referring to the taste of higher consciousness that is waiting for the Pilgrim, who feels a surge of joy and a powerful desire to be on the mountaintop. He feels completely light, as if he had wings and could fly.

When our travelers reach the top of the stairs, bad news comes—Virgil, the Pilgrim's beloved teacher, tells him he is leaving. Virgil, the symbol of reason, can go no further. He does not know how to reach the place where higher consciousness begins. Reason does not know about higher consciousness and, therefore, can no longer act as a guide. And, in addition, as Virgil explains, the Pilgrim no longer needs him.

Virgil's last words express the entire point of the climb up the mountain of purgatory:

I led you here with skill and intellect;
from here on, let your pleasure [for God] be your guide;
the narrow ways, the steep, are far below.

Behold the sun shining upon your [face],
behold the tender grass, the flowers, the trees…

Until those lovely eyes rejoicing come,
which, tearful, once urged me to come to you,
you may sit here or wander, as you please.

Expect no longer words or signs from me.
Now… your will [is] upright, wholesome, and free,…
I crown… you lord of yourself.

Lord of Yourself

Learning the mastery of the self through consciousness and choice is the purpose of Dante's mountain school. This mastery requires three skills: the basic ability (learned in hell) to witness rather than act on your negative patterns; the ability to name those patterns; and the discernment to give or refuse to give energy to any one of your patterns and to consciously choose to energize new patterns.

The third skill, discernment, is based on deciding whether a particular pattern increases suffering or increases peace. In Dantean terms, you must determine whether the pattern drops you down into hell or moves you up the mountain of purgatory toward experiences in paradise. Making that determination is the basis for every serious choice. There is no such thing as not choosing, for, as we have seen, even inertia and indifference have consequences.

When Virgil tells the Pilgrim his will is "upright, wholesome, and free," he is saying that his pupil has reached the stage of inner development where he can no longer tolerate causing more suffering. The Pilgrim has seen hell. He is convinced he never wants to go back. And his will—his ability to choose—has been liberated through the transformational work he did on the mountain of purgatory. His consciousness and choice are now educated enough to prepare him for the illuminations to come in paradise. At this point, those illuminations are all the Pilgrim is interested in. There was a beautiful John Martyn song years ago entitled *Don't Want to Know about Evil (Only Want to Know about Love)*. The Pilgrim only wants to know about love.

Dante uses increased lightness of being as a motif throughout the upward climb. Each time the Pilgrim's consciousness is liberated from a self-defeating pattern, one of his scars is healed and he feels lighter. At one point, you will recall, he mentions that it has become easier to climb the mountain than it was to walk on level ground. Dante is teaching us that the study of purgatory makes your life lighter and easier. For many of us, that in itself would be a religious experience.

In reality, however, the promise is much greater. Becoming lighter and easier is just the preparation for entering into higher states of consciousness. Feeling lighter, rising up, expanding into joy—these are not poetic metaphors but descriptions of actual experiences in states of illumination.

Beatrice is the guide to those states, and we will meet her next.

*"… Becoming lighter…
is just the preparation
for entering into higher
states of consciousness.
Feeling lighter, rising up,
expanding into joy…"*

CHAPTER SIX

First Contact With Wisdom

At the top of the mountain, the Pilgrim is immediately eager to explore his surroundings. Wandering about, he once more finds himself in the woods, but this wood is very different from the one at the entrance to hell, and rather than fear, it evokes in him a sense of beauty, peace, and clarity. On the other side of the stream, he sees a beautiful lady with light shining from her eyes, presiding over a world of peaceful innocence. The Pilgrim, however, is still on the opposite side of the stream, unable as yet to cross it.

The lady guides him along the bank to a spot where he sees, from across the water, the approach of a triumphal chariot pulled by a Griffin and bearing Beatrice. Upon his first sight of her, the Pilgrim says:

> *And instantly—though many years had passed*
> *since last I stood trembling before her eyes...*
>
> ...
>
> *My soul still felt... succumbing to her mystery*
> *and power, the strength of its enduring love.*

On a literal level, we must remember that the actual Beatrice had been the love of Dante's life, and, in that context, this meeting between his alter-ego, the Pilgrim, and the figure of Beatrice would, indeed, have been for him an impassioned reunion. In terms of Dante's teaching, however, we are witnessing the reunion of the Pilgrim's rational consciousness, now freed from its self-defeating patterns, with his wisdom mind, or, in Assagioli's words, his "higher self." It is a reunion rather than a first meeting because, in fact, we all carry our wisdom mind within us at all times. In the course of our daily lives, however, as we seek to meet the needs of our biological self and our social self, we lose track of our higher self to the point where, sadly, we even forget its existence.

Assagioli considered it "of fundamental importance" that we experience this reunion within ourselves. He developed many methods to help his patients and students have direct contact with their wisdom mind, and he saw the need for our educational systems to include information about this crucial part of our nature. He called it a "method of education toward wholeness."

The Pilgrim's own behavior tells us that he, himself, doesn't yet know what to make of this powerful reunion, how to use this resource within him. As he crosses the stream toward Beatrice, he is mentally paralyzed and confused: "I moved my lips, my throat striving to speak, but not a single breath of speech escaped," he tells us.

Beatrice challenges him: "Why...do you hesitate to question me, now that you are with me?"

And the Pilgrim responds: "My lady, you know all my needs, and how to satisfy them perfectly."

The Pilgrim is apparently hoping that she will save him from any more effort, but Beatrice begins his spiritual education with a wake-up call: "It is my wish that from now on you free yourself from fear and shame, and cease to speak like someone in a dream."

But why should the Pilgrim bother to wake up from his dream? Why, for that matter, should any of us bother to wake up? The name Buddha means "The One Who Is Awake," but most of us would prefer to be "The One Who Goes Back To Sleep." Life is difficult enough as it is. It would be easier to keep secretly dreaming and distracting ourselves than to wake up and acknowledge the root of our fear—the knowledge that we are all on a journey from birth through growth and decay, leading inevitably to death. We are happy enough to acknowledge birth and growth, but we are very unhappy with the notion of decay and death. An entire half of our life cycle makes us unhappy. It is a resilient human wish to be saved from this reality, and, too often, it is not until we are staring decay and death straight in the face that we feel the need to connect with our spiritual or higher self. When we do, however, that connection always brings the kind of peace and freedom from fear that, if we had been educated to recognize its existence, we would have sought much sooner in our life.

Variation on Wisdom Mind Practice

We taught you one wisdom mind practice in Chapter Two. You may want to refer back to it to begin experimenting with making this wisdom mind information personal and real for you. Here is a second form of the practice to try out. Read the instructions first.

1. Rest your hands on your belly and focus your attention on your hands.

2. It is natural for your attention to wander—just keep returning it to the sensations of your hands.

3. Now begin to notice the slight rise and fall of your breath in your belly... (Do this for a minute).

4. Now move your attention to your nose, noticing the sensations of your breathing... (Do this for a minute).

5. Now begin to imagine yourself in a natural setting where you feel safe and peaceful... This can be a place you have actually been to or one you create... Take a few moments to really sense being in this safe place...

6. Now notice or sense a figure walking towards you, a wisdom figure that represents the wisest part of you ... When the figure is

near you, allow yourself to communicate with this figure.

7. Be open to whatever happens.

The "safe place" aspect of this practice can contribute to your going into a deeper state of relaxation and inward focus. The addition of the "wisdom figure" turns your attention toward that higher part of your mind. Remember—your wisdom mind already exists. It is with you right now. Engaging in this practice will help you begin to notice it more easily. Be patient—you are developing a lifelong inner skill. It's alright if it takes time.

. . . .

Having seen so many people in such dire circumstances realize so much peace from making the connection to their spiritual selves, we cannot stress enough the benefits to be derived from its pursuit. One of our first and most profound experiences of how this can happen took place in the early 1980s during the height of the AIDS crisis when a former student named Charles called to tell us he was infected with HIV-AIDS. He was already extremely ill and in need of spiritual guidance, which he had been unable to find in the religion of his birth.

When we went to see him in his apartment, we had been working with him for a while to help him (as we had another AIDS patient, June, whom we've already discussed) understand and transform the way he was living with his fears. At that point he was in such discomfort that it was difficult to imagine how a simple change in consciousness could be of much help. In fact, however, that single session in his home provided him with a connection to his wisdom mind that was to help him profoundly throughout the rest of the dying process.

We led Charles into a relaxed, meditative state and then

through the wisdom mind practice. After twenty-five minutes in a deep, meditative state, during which there was palpable feeling of peace in the room, Charles slowly opened his eyes and began to relate what he had experienced.

> *I felt my body sink deep in the bed. I felt a great heaviness and peace. The itching went away, and it's still gone. I saw an image of a young man. I saw him become ill. I saw his flesh begin to fall off him, until a skeleton was all that was left.*
>
> *Then his flesh reappeared, and his life force returned. He was the same healthy young man I first saw. But soon, the flesh began to come off him again, his life force left him, and he became a skeleton again. At that point, I saw an old man behind him, and I realized that as the old man moved his hand to the left, the flesh came off the young man, and as the old man moved his hand to the right, the life came back to him. I watched this with great feelings of peace. I felt that I was being taught something very important. I can't even say the peace was in me, because by the time I was watching this I had absolutely no sense of my body at all. My body was gone. My body had dropped away. I was free; I was floating free. I had no fear at all. I was free.*

And with that, he closed his eyes and sank back into peace.

As we have said earlier, the images created by individual minds are extremely personal to the mind that created them. At the risk of violating our own principle, however, it would seem clear that Charles had connected with a state of higher wisdom that let him know he was connected to a spiritual realm beyond the physical, and that he was something more than the decaying body in which he presently lived.

As his illness progressed, Charles was hospitalized, and a few days later, he simply stopped communicating. Although he was not in a coma, he remained unresponsive to visitors who, quite naturally, assumed that this was a neurological or emotional consequence of his approaching death. We, however, sensed that Charles was not responding because he was determined to keep his mind focused inward.

Earlier, we had taught his closest friends how to help him through the meditative process, and he had made them promise to guide him to his inner wisdom when he was about to die. One night, as his friend Paul was leaving Charles's room, the nurse told him that she did not think Charles would live through the night. Remembering his promise, Paul returned to his friend's bedside and began to guide him as we had taught. Even though Charles remained unresponsive, Paul continued until he heard Charles say, "Don't worry. Charles is already gone." He died peacefully thirty minutes later.

Obstacles to Experiencing the Wisdom Mind

When Charles called us to ask for spiritual help, he had already received the harshest wake-up call anyone could imagine. Without that call, however, it can be harder for us to make the effort required to access that higher part of our nature. We have already seen how easy it was for the souls at the base of the mountain of purgatory to be distracted from seeking their true purpose, their connection with higher consciousness. And we know how easy it is for all of us to be distracted by our fears and self-defeating patterns of thought and behavior. Paradoxically, our need to soothe that fear is the greatest obstacle in the path of our connection to wisdom, when, in fact, making that connection is the only way to free ourselves from fear. There are, however, other obstacles as well.

One, also based on a kind of fear, is our stereotypical reaction to the notion of "hearing inner voices" or "seeing inner visions," which our culture has taught us to associate with mental illness, schizophrenia, dissociation from reality. As a result, we are afraid that if we admit to having such experiences people will think we are "crazy." Or maybe we will think we are crazy ourselves. Nothing, however, could be farther from the truth. We all, in fact, "see" and "hear" thoughts in our own minds every day. Doing that is how we process and "translate" information. In fact, it is a process that goes on in our minds virtually every moment of every day without our even being aware of it.

This unfounded fear that listening to our inner voices or images might mean we are crazy then leads to yet another obstacle—we doubt the authenticity of the experience itself. We find it difficult to believe that the insights we receive while in a state of higher consciousness could be of real significance. Time after time, we ourselves have seen patients open their eyes after meditation and say, "Where did *that* come from?" or "Did I make that up?" Precisely where within the brain/mind this inner wisdom comes from is still unknown. The astronaut Edgar Mitchell has pointed out that there is nothing super-natural, just very large gaps in our knowledge of what is natural.

And finally, there is the obstacle created by doubting that we will be able to do it. Many of our patients and students have come to us initially convinced that only "special" people are capable of spiritual experiences. The surest and most convincing way we have to prove that is not so is to help them connect with their own wisdom mind and experience higher consciousness for themselves. We know, however, from our more than forty years experience, that access to the wisdom mind is innate in all of us, regardless of education, maturity, cultural or religious background, or any other factor.

Children, in fact, have a natural connection to their inner

wisdom that is revealed in their art, their sometimes startlingly searching questions, and their natural affinity for love. It seems possible that the reason for this lies in the fact that they have not yet developed either the understanding of their own mortality that leads the rest of us to act out of fear rather than love or the cynicism that leads us to doubt the validity of what we are experiencing.

And yet, it is also true that even the most cynical and spiritually empty among us can reconnect with this part of themselves. One patient who proved the truth of this was a seventy-seven year old Holocaust survivor named Hilda who was facing a recurrence of breast cancer. Six years before, when she was first treated, her husband had been there to support her. But he had since died and now, even though her doctor was optimistic about her prognosis, Hilda did not think she would have the strength to go through it again on her own.

She told us that the emptiness she felt in herself had become frightening to her. "I have no strong feelings, no delights, no disappointments," she said. "Nothing matters. That is not life; that is a terrible stagnation. A sleep condition. I have to get out of this, but how?"

She then went on to tell us that as a young woman, before she left Germany, she would face her problems by cutting herself off from the world, going off by herself "to a lonely place in the heather or to an island" to retreat into herself, contemplate, and find the solution to whatever was bothering her.

After working with Hilda to help her recognize the fear-based thoughts that were preventing her from connecting with her wiser inner self, we suggested that she close her eyes, relax, and go back to the heather. This is how she described the experience.

I transported myself mentally to a suburban train heading to the heather. It's a beautiful summer day. The passing landscape is hazy, impressionistic. I get off at the heather station and walk down a long, gray, wide, very dusty road with deep ruts created by heavy wagons. There are no cars on this squalid road.

There are hardly any people. A few old fenced-in farmhouses to the right and left. Maybe no one lives in them. I walk on and see a little side path leading directly to the heather. I take the path and after a while even that ends. I go on, slowing down because of the thickness of the heather, and continue through this unlimited, unending heather field broken by only a few birch trees. This is real wilderness without man's interference.

Finally I sit down near some trees. How wonderful.

I decide to lie down and look at the cloudless, silky, pale blue sky, draped like a dome over the horizon. A very gentle wind caresses me and makes the little gray-greenish leaves of the birches move slightly, maybe talking together about the intruder—me— who lies so motionless. A few butterflies flutter around, busy bees hum and collect the nectar from the flowers of the heather and move gracefully with the wind. Everything is peaceful and disconnected from the daily crazy world. What a glorious day!

But I did not come here for adoration. I came to find my purpose, to feel better. I have to start searching. I fall into a deep sleep. I become a turtle, a little gray, insignificant, unnoticeable turtle, head inside under an impenetrable shell. Cut off from the lovely outer world.

I have to go down a chute, deep into the uncontrolled conflicts within me, past the vanity and finding excuses for everything I do, past the lies I tell myself, until I come to my own core, bare and naked, where my innermost soul begins. I sink deeper into sleep.

What is my problem? Is it the relationship between me and my family? Is it the relationship between friends and myself? Why do I suffer so much defeat despite wanting success? What is the destructive chemistry inside me?

I believe these are questions without easy answers. But to put the questions into words is already a cleansing, and awareness process.

Slowly I begin to wake up from this kind of trance. My hair sticks to my face. I smell the strong, good, earthy soil on which I lie and I love it. The sun is high in the sky now. Somehow I feel sweaty but good about myself, and I start walking again. Far away I see a herd of sheep with a shepherd. When I pass him, we greet one another.

Moving over this lovely, purplish, unending carpet of heather, I suddenly come to a big swimming pool filled with clear green water in the middle of nowhere. At the edge stands a short, white-haired, dark-skinned man who says hello. We talk a bit and he invites me to swim in his pool. I tell him I am a poor swimmer. I lose my breath easily from fear and would never let go of the ground beneath me.

He finally persuades me to swim across by promising to jump in immediately if I lose my breath or get panicky. Somehow I trust him and slowly submerge myself in the crystal clear water.

"Swim," he orders me. It is a command. I have to follow. I swim across, making sure he is still standing on the edge. I come to the far side of the pool and decide to stop.

"Turn and swim back—swim, swim. You can do it." I listen to him and do the exercise several times without stopping. I never did

such a long swim before in my life and I didn't have any breathing problems.

Finally I get out of the water and can hardly believe it was me who accomplished all this swimming. What kind of man was he to give me all this unexpected power and confidence? I don't know. I never see him again.

This achievement on that day gave me such an immense, beyond-any-words feeling of happiness that I will and never could forget it. I finish my trip by picking a huge bunch of heather for my grandmother, who preserves it for a year by pouring boiling water over it and keeping it dry in a vase.

When I open my eyes I really feel at peace. What a beautiful day!

Hilda was definitely not someone who would have believed in a wisdom level of the mind. Her life experience, in fact, had taught her quite the opposite—that there was very little of positive value to be found in human nature—and she probably could have filled an entire book with her negative opinions of religion and spirituality. And yet, despite her lack of belief, Hilda most assuredly connected with her wisdom mind that day and derived great benefit from it. Through her experience of higher consciousness, she was once more able to connect with a love of life and to believe in her own power. Ultimately, the experience is what gave her the strength to begin her treatment.

The Wisdom Mind and the World's Spiritual Traditions

The wisdom mind has long been recognized by all traditions that have developed an inner science of meditation, contemplation, or visualization. The oral and visual art of every spiritual tradition on earth includes references to it. So, as you begin your own journey to reconnect with it, you can do so with the confidence that you are joining a timeless, worldwide lineage of students who have wanted to know more about this important human resource.

The discovery of the wisdom mind occurs naturally as you sit quietly and witness what is going on inside you. When you first enter into a quiet state, you begin to notice all the various images, thoughts, and sensations passing through you. Among them, you will occasionally notice a particular thought or vision that moves you, that seems to expand your consciousness, or that brings you peace. You may not yet be able to pick it out among all the other inner phenomena you are experiencing, but, in time, if your body continues to relax, and your mind is able to let go of all your daily concerns and fears at least for a while, your wisdom mind will become more apparent. It was always there, but now you are able to notice it, just as Beatrice was always there at the top of the mountain, but it took the pilgrim a while to find her.

Three Qualities of the Wisdom Mind

The reward, as we hope you now realize, of doing the work of discovering your wisdom mind is to find the peace and joy that comes from recognizing this higher, more spiritual aspect of yourself. But what are the specific qualities that provide this elevation of your nature?

First of all, the wisdom mind contains highly organized, intimate information about you that might come to you as a deeply personal reference, a childhood nickname, or a long-forgotten event from your past, as when our patient Paul saw an image of himself as a lonely little boy on a bicycle. When that happens, you feel a sense of personal revelation, a release from confusion, a clarification of your life direction. You realize that there really is a deeper aspect of yourself that knows much more about you than your conscious mind, and that it is sending you information in the form of inner images, dreams, intuitions, and thoughts. In Italian renaissance painting, images are often depicted as being delivered by angels to humans, which was the artist's way of symbolizing knowledge moving from one level of our nature (our spiritual self) to another (our conscious self). In *The Divine Comedy*, Dante indicates his understanding of this kind of self-communication when Beatrice says of the Pilgrim, "I prayed that inspiration come to him through dreams and other means…"

Daniel was a patient of ours who gained this kind of understanding of himself by connecting with his inner wisdom. Daniel was a cocaine user who, like so many addicts, was unable to see or admit to himself that he was, in fact, addicted. We had been working with him to recognize and transform his addictive thought patterns and behavior for some time when he finally connected with a wisdom figure who allowed him to see himself clearly for the first time.

When we led him through the *Wisdom Mind* practice, he saw an old Asian man sitting inside a cabin and throwing ashes on a fire. When Daniel demanded that the figure explain the meaning of what he was doing, the old man just threw more ashes on the fire until there was only one small flame left. The life of the fire was being extinguished.

Again Daniel demanded to know the meaning of the man's

actions, and this time he put his finger next to his nose and said, "You do this."

"Do what?" Daniel shot back.

"The answer is right in front of your nose," the old man replied.

With that, Daniel began to sob because he had, for the first time, connected with a wiser part of himself that made him able to accept on a conscious level what he had known subconsciously all along.

The ability to bring those hidden thoughts and images to consciousness is one quality of the wisdom mind. Another, equally important, is that it is not driven by the passage of time. The thoughts and actions of our biological self, which is constantly aware of "time passing us by," are always predicated on that knowledge; our wisdom mind, however, shows no interest either in the passage of time or in how much time may be left for us. Nor does it care how long something takes. No matter how slowly you may be moving, if you are moving in the right direction, it will encourage you to keep going. One of the Bodhisattva vows of Zen Buddhism says, "Though the way is infinite, I vow to stay on it." Assagioli describes the time-frame of the wisdom mind this way: "From the eternal to the present for the future." In other words, the information we get in the present from that eternal or spiritual part of ourselves is guiding us to live with more peace and purpose in the future.

In order to do that, it has a third quality, which is that it emphasizes the expansion of love. Several years ago, when we were teaching a public seminar and guided a large room full of people through the *Wisdom Mind* exercise, one woman came up afterwards to tell us about the astonishing experience she just had. Apparently in all seriousness, she had asked her wisdom figure whether she should buy a new car and was shocked when the figure responded, "Will it help you to love?"

"… From the eternal to the
present for the future…"

On a much deeper level, however, our student Tom was struggling with being too judgmental of both himself and other people. "Put me in a social setting," he said, "and all I do is look around, finding fault with everyone. It's a nonstop monologue in my head. And then sometimes the judgment turns on me, tearing me down and evaluating my life as a failure and me as a loser." When he decided to ask his wisdom mind to help him become more loving, this is what he experienced.

> *I saw in front of me an ancient Mayan temple. It was deserted and overgrown. I approached it with anticipation, and I gladly began to climb up the steps. When I got to the top, I had a breathtaking view of the surrounding valley.*
>
> *As I turned, I saw a huge fire emanating from the center of the platform. The flame must have been six feet in diameter and spitting flames thirty feet into the air. I moved closer and noticed a wooden bench situated there that seemed to indicate that I was to sit down. A figure emerged from the flame. He wasn't flesh and bones but simply fire. He stepped onto a plank and stood about four feet from where I was sitting. It felt strange, but I started talking to him. I told him about my judgmentalism and how isolated it makes me feel.*
>
> *The first thing he reminded me of was that my acceptance of others was also the work of accepting myself. I then told him that I wanted to be able to look at people in my life, strangers included, and be able t see them with love and compassion. How do I do this, I asked?*
>
> *He said a few things back. One was that I could use the image of the acorn and its development into a mighty oak. I took this to mean that I should see people as more than they were at the*

moment, that I should trust in their unseen potential.

I found myself trying this out in my imagination. I called up images of different people in my life. I stood face to face with them and remembered the acorn. I experienced myself feeling differently towards them. I felt less energy in my judgments. Small amounts of love and acceptance began to bubble up.

To go further, I chose a complete stranger on the street. I chose someone whom I would typically write off with judgments and stereotypes. When an image of this person appeared, I got the idea to look at her from the point of view of the wisdom figure. I left my body and allowed my consciousness to merge into the wisdom figure so that I was looking out through his eyes. A wonderful thing began to happen. Slowly, words became audible within me and I found myself going from a position of dismissal to one of openness and curiosity. I found myself filling with thoughts of compassion. I couldn't sustain it very long but I had an experience of what I was hoping for.

I thanked the wisdom figure. He invited me to come with him on a short journey and then jumped into the fire and disappeared. I felt stuck, and then I jumped into the flames, too. It didn't hurt at all. My body disappeared and I experienced myself as only awareness. In the fire, I saw a blue light like at the bottom of a candle's yellow flame. I stared at it a long time. I don't remember having any thoughts at all. What followed were several bursts of light waves emanating from the flame. It looked like something from a Star Trek movie. There was no explosion, just this gigantic wave of light that went out from this tiny blue flame and traveled to the ends of the universe and farther. I could see it all the way out there. The next thing I knew, I entered into the flame and "caught a ride" on the next wave.

When I arrived at the farthest reaches of the universe I could still see the blue flame of the candle all the way back where I had started. I felt an intense expansiveness and energy. I wasn't sure if I could contain it, but I stayed with it for as long as I could. I looked around at one point and saw that the entire room was connected with this energy and light. I didn't realize that I had opened my eyes.

I immediately began to question: What was that? Did that just happen to me? Did I just go somewhere?

Tom's connection with his wisdom mind not only allowed him to see "with loving eyes" but also to have a truly illuminating experience of the loving unity that expands to encompass the entire universe. If you compare his experience to the experiences of Nancy, the patient we discussed in Chapter Two, you will see how similar and yet individual are these illuminative wisdom mind experiences.

When we consider the three qualities of the wisdom mind—its ability to give us information about ourselves, its disregard for the passage of time, and its emphasis on the expansion of love—we are able to define this aspect of ourselves as a higher organizing process of our brain that has evolved to increase our ability to expand love in the future. If that definition is correct, cultivating the wisdom mind can be seen as a profoundly revolutionary step in your self-development—an empowering and liberating process that aligns you with a deep truth about life and your purpose in it.

Your own Beatrice, your own higher self, your own wisdom mind, is ready to become part of your life right now.

The Function of Doubt

It is not only natural but, in fact, essential, that at this point you bring your rational mind to question virtually everything we have told you so far about wisdom mind experiences. Just as the Pilgrim was doing when he was reunited with Beatrice, you are embarking on a spiritual education, and it is vital that your rational mind be honored as you travel this spiritual path. Other spiritual teachers may have taught you otherwise. Some may have suggested that your rationality is an obstacle to spirituality. A few may even have suggested that it's necessary to annihilate the ego in order to achieve spirituality. But such suggestions deny just about everything that is true about human nature.

You *need* your rational mind to integrate your spiritual experiences into your everyday life. And if you cannot do that, you will not be able to benefit from their true value, which is to bring more peace and joy into the life you have.

In the following chapter we will see how the Pilgrim questions Beatrice, trying to use his rationality in order to understand the states of higher consciousness she is teaching him to experience. Her job as his teacher is, as ours is with you, to help him go beyond rationality to experience illumination—and then to reintegrate those illuminative experiences into his life as a whole.

CHAPTER SEVEN

Developing A Relationship With Your Wisdom Mind

Among all things, however disparate,
there reigns an order...

and in this order all created things...
move... across the vast ocean of being,
...each endowed with its own instinct as its guide.

...this is the moving force in mortal hearts,
this is what binds the earth and makes it one.

----- Beatrice

To understand the true nature of illuminative experiences, the Pilgrim, like all of us, must learn to quiet and relax his rational mind long enough to begin building a relationship with his wisdom mind. In terms of Dante's poem that means he must learn to trust what Beatrice has to teach him. He is an eager student, but also a difficult one because, in his own eagerness, he is constantly trying to use his rational mind to interpret experiences that are beyond rational understanding.

The Experience of More

The way to develop a relationship with your wisdom mind and thereby open yourself up to transformational, illuminative experiences is not, as we have said all along, to in any way deny or destroy the rational part of your nature, which is necessary for daily functioning in the real world.

It is the rational mind that brings order to our actions and allows us to accomplish daily tasks. Our rational mind can also help us to conquer many fears and superstitions. In fact, for Dante's lost Pilgrim, it was Virgil, the rational aspect of his mind, who had helped him to overcome his fear of the journey to hell and who guided him to his first meeting with Beatrice.

Discovering our inner wisdom is not, then, a way to get rid of or reject any part of who we are; rather it is a way to expand our own understanding of who we are in order to become more than we were. To help the Pilgrim do that, Beatrice must honor and satisfy his rational mind while, at the same time, she provides him with a way to relax and release those rational thought processes in order to access a higher, more spiritually aware part of his being.

The Teacher and the Wisdom Mind

By making Beatrice an actual, physical character who personifies both inner wisdom and the teacher of wisdom, Dante is using her to fulfill a dual role. The wisdom mind resides within each and every one of us, but sometimes we require help from a teacher to access that capacity within ourselves. As the Pilgrim's teacher, Beatrice knows more than her student; as an aspect of himself that he has yet to explore, she represents his own untapped knowledge.

As a teacher, Beatrice is first and foremost a role model. She exemplifies the inner peace her student is seeking to achieve, thereby reflecting the benefits of the knowledge she is teaching. In other words, she does not just talk the talk; she also walks the walk.

When we guide our own students and patients to access and develop a relationship with their wisdom mind, we lead them to imagine their own Beatrice. In effect, through guided meditation, we help people do what Dante did in creating the character of Beatrice. We show them how to mentally personify an aspect of themselves so that they can more

easily become familiar with it, dialogue with it, and come to trust the
wisdom it has to impart.

Seeing Through Beatrice's Eyes

Shortly after they meet, Beatrice, through her example, provides
the Pilgrim with his first experience of illumination:

I saw Beatrice...facing left,
her eyes raised to the sun—no eagle ever
could stare so fixed and straight into such light...

Like a ray, her act poured through my eyes
into my mind and gave rise to my own [act]:
I stared straight at the sun...

And suddenly it was as if one day
shone on the next—as if [God]
had decked the heavens with a second sun.

And Beatrice stood there, her eyes fixed...
entranced, and now
my eyes, withdrawn from [the light] were fixed on her.

For that brief time, the Pilgrim saw through Beatrice's eyes—
as Nancy, in Chapter Two saw through the monk's eyes and Tom saw
through the eyes of the old wise man at the Mayan Temple—the "light"
of higher consciousness.

What Beatrice has been teaching him here is the beginning of
contemplation—how to focus consciousness at a spiritual level, to gaze,

in other words, into the light of illumination by which we are able to "see" aspects of reality that are not readily noticeable in daily life. The Pilgrim was able to do this, but he was not able to maintain that gaze for long, nor was he able to explain what it was he had just experienced.

The contemplative state of mind, as it is developed, perceives reality at subtler and subtler levels, and the imagination—the image-making function of our mind—creates images of these subtler perceptions. One of the subtlest perceptions of all is to apprehend the life energy that pervades all of reality, and that energy is commonly represented in our imagination as the perception of light. The world's spiritual art abounds with images of halos, light beaming from eyes, light surrounding bodies, light shooting out of the palms of hands. All of these are representations of the experience of inner light—the light into which the Pilgrim and Beatrice were gazing.

An Indescribable Lightness of Being

At the conclusion of his first experience of illumination, the Pilgrim feels himself being pulled up into the light and asks, "Which part of me rose?" This is very much the same confused reaction expressed by St. Paul in 2 Corinthians 12 about his own conversion experience: "I was caught up in paradise…whether in the body, or out of the body, I cannot tell."

Again, this sense of rising up into the light is both an image universally depicted in spiritual or religious painting and one that has been frequently reported by those who have had mystical experiences. It is a pictorial representation of the experience of rising to a higher level of consciousness.

In answer to the Pilgrim's question, Beatrice tells him:

Lightning
never sped downward from its home as quick
as you are now ascending to your own.

She is offering more than a metaphorical explanation for his experience. Lightning literally does descend from the sky, and consciousness, once it is liberated from rational thought, rises up into the spiritual light.

Speaking further of the effect the experience has had on him, the Pilgrim says:

I saw a great expanse of heaven ablaze...
The revelation of this light...
inflamed me with such eagerness to learn...
as I had never felt before;

and she who saw me as I saw myself,
ready to calm my agitated mind,
began to speak before I asked my question.

The Desire for More

The Pilgrim is having early tastes of the spiritual dimension of reality, and he is very excited by what he has experienced. He wants to understand it and know more about it, but he is trying to do that by using his rational mind, which, as his teacher, his wisdom mind, Beatrice reminds him, is not the way to spiritual wisdom:

You have yourself to blame for burdening
your mind with misconceptions that prevent

[you] from seeing clearly what you might have seen.

She knows, as do the mystics who have sung about it in poetry and song, that the experience itself is the point. Trying to analyze and explain it, although a natural enough impulse for one who has not yet formed a trusting relationship with the power of his wisdom mind, is to return our attention to our personality, to our own usual mental activity rather than the deeper reality the experience has brought us.

That is not to say, however, that we cannot engage in a process that will allow us to replicate and gain a better understanding of what we have experienced. In fact, that is not only what we all must do but also what we naturally desire to do once we have had a "taste" of the kind of bliss those moments of illumination can bring. Andrew, who was one of our students, has described the illuminative moment that started him on his own path of spiritual study.

> *At thirty-one I was lost. I had a bad job and a good family, but in my soul, in my essential feeling of myself, I was lost. Then something happened to change everything.*
>
> *We were in the Adirondack Mountains on vacation. We rented a canoe and went out on Lake George. Suddenly, the bright day turned black, the wind whipped up, and thunder and lightning started to crash down on us. The lake became agitated, and our canoe was turned over by the waves.*
>
> *Thrown into the water with our two little kids, my wife and I got hold of them and frantically swan to shore. The terror continued. The lightning was slashing into the trees, setting them on fire over our heads, and fiery tree branches began to fall around us. We had no place to go. I suddenly realized that we were going to die.*

Dying wasn't a thought. It was a deep-in-the-bone reality. I felt it through my whole body. I looked at my family with the absolute certainty that all we had left was a few seconds of living. Our time had come. In that instant, something deep, deep in me released, and I went into total bliss. Bliss was blazing out of my eyes and out of all the pores of my skin. I was shattered, I was gone. I was bliss in love with everything.

I heard, "Run!" Still in bliss, I was following my wife and son and carrying my daughter as we ran toward a deeper part of the woods. My wife had seen, in the light of the lightning, the shape of a house. We got to it and opened a side door just as the storm turned into huge hailstones crashing down. Later that day, we would see all the cars in town with big dents in their roofs and hoods.

The house was dark. We heard someone coming from far away. We called out that we meant no harm and were just trying to get in out of the storm. A very old woman appeared at the other end of the room. We apologized again for breaking into her house, but she seemed serene and undisturbed. She told us to sit down and wait for the storm to abate, and then she turned, feeling her way along the wall toward the door through which she had entered. We realized then that she was blind.

In the dark room, we could see electricity shooting out of the electrical outlets. The air outside was alive with the electricity of the lightning. A man came into the room, did not even ask who we were, and excitedly told us that he had seen balls of lightning rolling across the fields. He then went to the other room to check on the old woman. The hailstones were still smashing down.

Sitting in the dark room, soaking wet, shivering, afraid to move because of the electrical sparks, I felt a sweet residue of bliss still *with me. I was incredibly happy that my wife and children were safe and would have lives that lasted longer than this afternoon. But for me, I had experienced myself one hundred percent set to die. My wife had saved us with her fierce protective energy by making us run to the house, while I had only stood there surrendering and blissed out. I had to admit that I had given up.*

When the storm passed, we got up to leave and yelled "thank you" into the dark recesses of the old woman's house, but we heard nothing in return. As we made our way back to the road so that we could hitchhike into town, I looked around me. Whatever thoughts I'd had were now gone. Whatever opinions I once had were now gone. Whatever identity I had shaped for myself was now gone. I knew only that I knew nothing. My mind was as empty as the road. Nothing on it. Nothing going anywhere. No coming, no going, nothing. And then, completely by itself, a single clear thought came and sat in my mind: I must understand. I must understand. I knew I knew nothing, and I had to understand. The next day, I began to look for a spiritual teacher.

Like the Pilgrim, Andrew had an experience that he knew was completely different from anything he had experienced before. While he was having it, he was experiencing the feeling of being at one with all of creation. In retrospect, he wanted to understand what had happened in that moment; his spiritual seeking had begun.

"Bliss" may be a feeling beyond the capacity of words to describe, but it is one we all naturally long for even when we do not know it; it is that indescribable something we somehow sense is missing from our life. And once having felt it, we cannot help but deeply long to experience it again.

The Teaching of the Wisdom Mind

Nancy responded to her first introduction to her wisdom mind by saying, "What the hell was that?" And Tom asked "Did I just go somewhere?" These are their contemporary equivalents of Dante's Pilgrim asking Beatrice, "Which part of me rose?" They are all trying to understand what they have experienced.

The Pilgrim cannot let go of his need to know more, and he says to Beatrice: "I wonder how I can rise through these light bodies here."

And she responds, the Pilgrim tells us, with the loving exasperation of a parent.

> She sighed … when she heard my question
> and looked at me the way a mother might
> hearing her child in his delirium.

Because she is both his teacher and the personification of his own inner wisdom, Beatrice knows that the Pilgrim has within himself the power to discover the answers to his own questions. She wants to lead him to those answers, as any good guide or teacher would, but she also knows that he must come to an understanding of his own inner wisdom for himself. Her role is to help him bring his own spirituality to the surface of his life.

Although, from a literary point of view, Dante's descriptions of the experience of illumination might be taken as poetic metaphors, they are, in actuality, very accurate accounts of higher states of consciousness. Since higher consciousness is a state that must be experienced to be truly understood, we assume that Dante himself had known such illuminative moments for himself.

We can imagine the poet alone in his room, perhaps in a melancholic moment, conjuring up an image of the lost Beatrice and carrying on a mental dialogue with that image, and her responding, again in his imagination.

When we ask students and patients to imagine a wisdom figure, it is not unusual for them to also "see" the image of someone who has passed away and who they can imagine as now having knowledge of what is, after all, life's greatest mystery—what happens when we die? If our imagined scenario is correct, Dante would have spent many hours over many years communing with his wisdom mind, an act that would have raised his consciousness above his fears and his rational thinking and would have opened him to the personal experiences of illumination that he describes.

It would be natural, too, that Dante would have had questions about those illuminations, since that is the first reaction any of us have after the illumination has passed and we have returned to our usual way of thinking and perceiving. Our questions do not necessarily come because of any confusion about the illumination itself: the experience is always self-evident, with its own positive feelings and intuitive understanding. Rather, our questions come afterwards, from the fact that we are generally uneducated and inexperienced about our natural potential for higher consciousness. We ask questions because we are still finding our way into this unknown part of our nature. It makes perfect sense, then, that Dante's Pilgrim asks so many questions of Beatrice. As we will see later on, his questions become fewer as he has more experience of the higher states and is better able to let the experiences themselves be his teacher. The dialogue Dante describes as occurring between Beatrice and the Pilgrim almost surely represents Dante's own process of understanding and accepting of his higher nature.

The Need for Faith

In our work with our modern pilgrim Nancy in Chapter Two, we saw that she was initially afraid to let go of the rock wall and take flight with the monk. Letting go of our rational fears and our self-protective behaviors in order to experience the freedom of higher consciousness can be a frightening proposition, and Dante acknowledges that when he says, speaking directly to the reader:

> *All who in your wish to hear my words*
> *have followed thus far in your little boat...*
>
> *go back now while you still can see your shores;*
> *do not attempt the deep: it well could be*
> *that [in] losing me, you would be lost yourselves.*

But he also understands that those who are truly seekers will not be deterred, and to those he says:

> *Those few of you who from your youth have raised*
> *Your eager mouths in search of angels' bread*
> *... always hungering,*
>
> *you may, indeed, allow your boat to sail*
> *the high seas...*

Opening ourselves up to the power of the wisdom mind, letting go of our fears, is, at first, like launching a small vessel into uncharted waters. It is not until we become familiar with the spiritual territory, our own higher states of consciousness, that we can trust ourselves to be safe there.

The Pilgrim trusts Beatrice to captain his ship. The longer they are together, the more he comes to trust her, and to accept the validity of what he is experiencing:

> *We seemed to be enveloped in a cloud*
> *as brilliant, hard, and polished as a diamond*
> *struck by a ray of sunlight. That eternal,*
>
> *Celestial pearl took us into itself,*
> *receiving us as water takes in light,*
> *its indivisibility intact.*

The Pilgrim is beginning to struggle less as he merges into the light. The celestial pearl takes him in, and he becomes one with it. His experiences of illumination are becoming more natural to him. Since nothing "bad" has happened to him as a result of what he has been experiencing—his boat has neither run aground nor been lost at sea— he is now better able to relax and surrender to his initiation into the "vast ocean of being," that is, into our greater nature. The more we are able to relax the grasp of our rational mind and trust in our wisdom mind, the easier it will be for us to access the illuminating experiences it has to offer us.

Let Go

There is a deceptively simple exercise to help you relax your personality and your body so that your wisdom mind can be more noticeable and accessible to you. This exercise relies on the quiet power of words—a power we talked about when we suggested the use of evocative words and affirmations as transformational exercises in

Chapter Five. We teach it to all of our patients and students because it is both so effective and so easy to use at any time and in any place.

Among its many benefits, it can be used to reduce anxiety, to prepare ourselves to focus better, to ready ourselves for meditation, to shift our mood or feelings if we are in an argument or getting too worried. We routinely use it as a warm-up for imagery and meditation with anyone who is feeling distracted or preoccupied. When you first read the instructions, the practice may sound too easy and too simple to actually work. We strongly encourage you to try it, however, and to bring its benefits into your life.

Read the instructions first, and then try it for yourself.

1. Close your eyes...allow your body to give way into the chair...

2. Now, in the privacy of your mind, begin to repeat this three-word phrase –

3. First say your name, and then follow it with the words "let go."

4. Say the three-word phrase over and over in your mind, at a relatively slow pace, for about three minutes.

5. Then let go of the phrase itself and rest in the silence in your mind. When the silence passes, open your eyes.

A frequent question that comes up around this practice is what to let go of. You do not need to try to let go of anything in particular— the phrase itself will do the work for you. If you hear questions in your mind or feel confused while you are in the midst of doing the exercise, just return to the phrase itself. Sometimes, once you are fairly focused on it, the phrase will disappear by itself and there will be a quiet in your mind. You will have naturally arrived at Step 5—just rest in the silence.

What Does It All Mean—The Impulse for Truth

Having illuminative experiences such as the Pilgrim's proves to us that we are capable of freeing ourselves from preoccupation with habitual patterns of thought and expanding into subtler states of perception. But the non-ordinary experiences themselves are not really the point. The real point is to arrive at a deeper truth.

The Pilgrim, at this early stage of his spiritual development, is still fascinated by extraordinary nature of the experiences themselves, but Beatrice, who is far more spiritually mature, knows that the phenomenon of seeing the light, while it is interesting, is not all there is. She needs to teach the Pilgrim to see beyond the light itself in order to penetrate its meaning.

The Pilgrim is trying very hard, but his experiences are occurring faster than his mind can understand them:

Before my eyes, appeared a vision,
absorbing my attention so completely…

As faint an image as comes back to us
Of our own face reflected in a smooth
Transparent pane of glass…

I saw [faces] there, eager to speak…
I turned to find out whose they were,

and saw no one. I looked around again
into the radiance of my sweet guide

whose sacred eyes were glowing as she smiled.

Beatrice, who realizes the Pilgrim is about to ask a question to which she already knows the answer, says, "You should not be surprised to see me smile at your naive reaction…You do not trust the evidence you first saw…You turn away to stare at emptiness."

What she is trying to help him understand is that the light is more than simply a visual event, that there is a particular *quality* in the light experience, and that is the energy within it, which is the energy of love. He, however, keeps turning away from what he is experiencing in order to question it before he has had a chance to experience its full impact on him. His reaction is analogous to what happens when we "blank out" on what someone is telling us because it sounds like bad news: Our biological self and our social self, focused on safety and functioning, do not want to hear anything that threatens them. This impulse is the same mechanism by which unrelated thoughts or impulses intrude into the mind during a meditative state. We have already discussed the fact that many people find themselves, in the midst of a meditation, experiencing the urge to make a phone call or check their calendar or do some other, totally mundane task. These thoughts are our biological and social selves short-circuiting the experience because the experience is of an unknown nature and is, therefore, initially threatening to these selves, which have, for our entire lifetime, been trying to gain some control over reality.

At this point, the Pilgrim is virtually immobilized by his own confusion:

Between two equal equidistant foods
A man, though free to choose, would starve to death
Before he put his teeth in either one.

I did not speak, but written on my face
was my desire, all of my questioning.

Beyond Images

The Pilgrim has now had several experiences of his consciousness merging into a higher state, a subtler energy, and the image-making function of his mind—his imagination—has been making images out of the experiences. These are the same images—of light, of a physical rising—that, as we have said, artists have relied on to depict spiritual states. The image is helpful in representing our experience in our mind, in our memory, but the image is not the truth of the experience. Assagioli put this learning into a simple developmental schema: "Energies descend into images, and images into words." A Zen expression also clarifies this understanding quite beautifully and succinctly as, "The finger pointing at the moon is not the moon."

The Pilgrim he has reached an important time in his spiritual education. Beatrice is going to try to take his understanding beyond the images he is seeing:

I speak as one must speak to minds like yours
which apprehend only from your sense perception...

For this same reason, Scripture condescends
to your intelligence, attributing...
hands and feet to God;
and the [church] presents to you [angels]
with human features.

With this comment, Dante is reminding us that the words and images of religion are not the actual experiences. The image is different from the reality it represents, and at some point in our spiritual development we have to move beyond the representations to the underlying truths. Our wisdom mind, represented by Beatrice, already knows this, and it tries to guide our rational mind to feel safe enough to relax into the unity we are, in fact, already living in.

The Nature and Function of Questions

The more he learns, the better the Pilgrim begins to understand why it is he is questioning so much of what he is experiencing. He is gaining insight into the nature and function of questioning itself. Questions are quests, and the mind knows there is something much greater to comprehend:

I see man's mind cannot be satisfied
Unless it be illumined by that Truth
Beyond which there exists no other truth.
Within that Truth, once man's mind reaches it,
It rests like a wild beast within its den.
And it can reach it…

So at the foot of truth, like shoots,
our doubts spring up; this is a natural force
urging us to the top from height to height.

And this gives me the courage that I need…
to ask about a truth that is not clear to me.

He is getting to the root of what it is that is fueling his impulse to question, and that is the impulse for truth. It is an impulse innate in all of us, in our relationships, in our families, in the organizations to which we belong, and in governments. When we see a violation of what we know to be true, we call it injustice, and it angers us because it disturbs our innate impulse for truth, which we cannot deny or suppress no matter how hard we may try.

The Pilgrim says that after hearing her student's words:

Beatrice looked at me, her eyes
sparkling with love and burning so divine,
my strength ... surrendered to her power.

She is happy that he has finally gained this degree of understanding, and he, having recognized the reason for his questions, has become a true student, finally willing to give up all control to his teacher in order to arrive at the object of his quest, which is, as it is for all of us, the deeper truth. The truth which is the underlying unity that exists above, below, all around and inside the separate things and beings we see at the superficial level of perception. The need to control derives from our fear; the willingness to give up control indicates that we are letting go of those fears, which happens naturally as we get closer to the truth of our connection with the eternal loving energy of the universe.

Beatrice acknowledges her student's progress in this regard by saying,

I can see how into your mind already
There shines Eternal Light which ...
Once it is seen, forever kindles love.

The Loving Force

That "Eternal Light," the light of illumination, was personified by Dante as Lucie. The loving force it reveals is personified as Mary. Mary is an image or symbol that may be irrelevant to some people. However, the divine feminine loving force she personifies is very real. And because it is real, we must all find a way to honor it for ourselves as a part of our deeper reality.

In 1995, when we traveled with a group of people who were going to adopt children from an orphanage in China, we spent a week deeply experiencing that field of divine loving energy. There were nine families in the group and nine little girls who would come home to America. Each family held a photograph of a little girl close to their hearts, a picture of *their* child.

After months and months of applications and bureaucratic procedures, this journey across the Pacific Ocean was the culmination of a search to satisfy a deep longing. We could feel the air charged with the energy of hope and expectancy. The extraordinary moments when the children were brought out of the orphanage and received by their parents released an outflow of intense love, tears, and joy.

During that week in China, we witnessed and felt a fierce protectiveness towards the children. Parents were noticing and adoring every little burp and coo, fussing over and caring for rashes and cradle cap, colds and tears. Their love was enormous, a force of nature. Various members of the group commented on how completely shocked they were by the ongoing intensity of it. One father, holding his little Joy in his arms, his eyes filling with tears, said, "I thought I was doing this for my wife, but I can't believe how in love I am with this kid," and then he broke down sobbing.

The loving force can rise in you in the simplest moments, and you can cultivate your inner ability to open to it more and more. You find out, in time, that you are not discovering it but that it is discovering a way to be expressed through you. It is the universal energy each individual is responsible for bringing into the world.

The Next Step

Now we are at a crossroads. Having been introduced to the underlying unity of all reality through our spiritual level of perception, our social self will, nevertheless, continue to see things as separate. The feeling of separation slowly but surely reasserts itself as our primary vision of life because it is so conditioned in us and so easy to describe. You are you, they are they, and it appears quite obvious that we are all separate and different. The underlying unity is far more difficult to hold on to and to describe because it is everywhere in everything. Unity cannot be divided up into separate words, even though we have admittedly tried to do just that in order to convey its importance to you. Dante describes the difficulty most beautifully when he says that in angelic consciousness you "do not have divided thought."

When we cross over, temporarily, from our separateness and enter into the unity, we know again that the unity is not an abstraction or a metaphor but an objectively real, universal, pervading energy. When we come back from such an experience, however, we can only try to describe it in the language of our own culture. And, because of that, spiritual descriptions deriving from different cultures may appear to be describing different experiences. In fact, however, there is only one universal experience that is being repeatedly discovered—it is the experience of the underlying, factual unity of all reality. And how do we know it is worthwhile to discover this for ourselves? The bliss, the joy, and the knowledge tell us so.

In the following chapters we will help you to have your own breakthrough experiences into unity as we describe how Beatrice led the Pilgrim to his.

CHAPTER EIGHT
Experiences In Higher Consciousness

States of higher consciousness are temporary experiences, sometimes lasting just a few seconds of clock time, during which a deeper level of reality becomes illuminated for us. We see and feel the eternal force, intelligence, and energy that animates all things and all beings, including ourselves. During those few seconds we, too, feel timeless and realize our most intimate participation in the web of life. What stays with us after having such an experience is the feeling of its importance for everyone and the desire to transmit knowledge of its existence to everyone.

Both Dante and Assagioli experienced many states of higher consciousness and both dedicated their lives to passing the knowledge of these states on to others. Dante spent the last eleven years of his life writing the story of his path to higher consciousness in order to help lead people "from misery to bliss," and Assagioli spent his sixty-five years of professional practice discovering and perfecting the best methods for achieving the experience of higher consciousness so that he could teach them to his patients, his students, and colleagues around the world. Dante's personal story resulted, of course, in *The Divine Comedy*, and Assagioli's work became the foundation of psychosynthesis.

The words we and others have used to describe it cannot even come close to capturing the experience of higher consciousness, and even Dante, poetic genius though he was, complained frequently in *The Divine Comedy* that his words were powerless to describe the immensity of those illuminations.

Therefore, there are two jobs we have in guiding you into higher consciousness. The first is to give you words and understanding about these "higher" experiences, and the second is to teach you methods you can use to experience them for yourself.

These methods have come to us from many sources, from our personal experience, and, most of all, from our teacher Assagioli.

Assagioli was clear about the objective reality of higher consciousness. In addressing the doubts of those critics who questioned it, he commented that, "One has to create the conditions for having the experience, and scientists up to now have not taken the trouble to do that."

How do we create the conditions for an illumination? The first thing to understand is that an illumination can, and often does, occur spontaneously without any preparation. The religious writer, C.S. Lewis, wrote *Surprised by Joy* to describe just such a spontaneous experience. For us the very fact that people of all cultures in every period of history, have had them is, in itself, proof of their objective reality. Take a moment to think back over your own life—have you had such a moment of illumination, a transcendent feeling, a sense of deep soulful connection to the world? You may want to refer back to our *Time of Meaning* exercise in Chapter Three as a way of stirring your memory.

Creating The Conditions

Clearly, neither we nor anyone else can guide you to have a spontaneous experience, but we can show you how to deliberately create the conditions to have experiences of higher consciousness. If you make the deliberate choice to create those conditions, you will be stepping on the same path Dante, Assagioli, and countless others have traveled to explore and discover deeper levels of reality.

Many people seem to believe that one would have to meditate for years in order to experience higher consciousness, but that simply isn't true. Meditation is only one of the many methods available for creating the conditions that lead to higher consciousness, and, in fact, it has been our experience that many people actually create those conditions not through meditation but through either engagement (as either creator or contemplator) of a work of art or engaging in service to others.

The reason for this, we believe, is that both these activities require that we temporarily suspend our interest in ourselves and surrender ourselves to another person's experience—as the Pilgrim surrendered himself to Beatrice. We either open ourselves to the artist's inspiration or we open ourselves to the situation and feelings of someone in need. The act of temporarily surrendering the self creates the conditions for entering a state of higher consciousness because it liberates us from our habitual patterns and frees our consciousness for the experience of something new.

That is why the self-knowledge you gain from descending into hell and climbing the mountain of purgatory is so important. Without that self-knowledge, the energy of your consciousness remains trapped in negative states of being and is not free to expand into new levels of reality. By continuing to practice liberation from those negative states, you will, therefore, be more able to move on to the rewarding and pleasurable higher states we are now exploring together.

The Path of the Arts

Assagioli spoke of artistic inspiration as a downflowing of some essential insight or truth about the universe into our conscious awareness and then expressing that downflow through some form of art. He used Dante's own words as a prime example of one who had been so inspired: "I am one who, when love breathes on me, notices, and in the manner that [love] dictates within, I utter words."

Leonard Bernstein wrote about experiencing this downflowing of joy while conducting an orchestra: "...it takes minutes before I know where I am—in what hall, in what country, or who I am. Suddenly, I become aware that there is clapping, that I must bow. It's the same sort of ecstasy as the trance you are in when you are composing…You don't know what time it is or what's going by."

Most of us can probably recall a special moment when a film, a painting, a photographic image, a dance performance, a poem, a piece of music, an architectural space, or a sculpture took us into this downflowing of joy because the artist's inspiration engaged us, too. But art can just as certainly take us down into sadness and fear, or to a personal confrontation and transformation, both of which also contribute to our spiritual growth.

Laurie, a student of ours, gave us the notes she made in her diary after experiencing just such an art-inspired illumination while traveling in Rome. Her experience was both spontaneous and deliberate, in the sense that, although the illumination itself came as a spontaneous surprise, she had deliberately traveled to a place filled with inspiration, thereby creating the condition that allowed it to occur.

Entering St. Peter's. Experiencing its hugeness. Awesome. Is this structure designed to humble me? I experience myself resisting it. All vertical and overbearing. I feel like I'm in the land of giants. There is beauty present, but it feels remote and cold. Perhaps when it is filled with thousands of worshippers, it will warm up and soften.

I find myself drawn to the side chapel where Michelangelo's Pieta is displayed. I can't approach it—it is behind a glass wall, protected from any threat of attack. It draws my gaze despite the barrier, and I feel myself pulled towards it. I'm first drawn to the Virgin Mary's face. It is the face of a young girl not older than adolescent. Soft, delicate, yet serenely sad, wise beyond her years, yet innocent and confused by the situation she is in.

My eyes survey the rest of the sculpture. The soft, translucent white of the marble, the folds of drapery and the large figure of the dead Christ draped across Mary's lap. This lifeless body is much too large to be Mary's child. I've seen many Pietas—paintings and sculptures—why are there tears in my eyes? I'm drawn back to Mary's delicate face. I can't turn away. Why is she so young and innocent? Certainly Michelangelo knew how to sculpt an older woman. No, there is a reason she appears like this. Suddenly I understand. This image is about a human experience. Mary is a mother whose child has been killed. Is a person ever old enough to not be completely vulnerable to this loss?

When I first became a mother, I remember being frightened by the intensity of my protective instincts and the degree to which thoughts of my son being harmed terrified me. I feel joined to Mary's face. I can see myself and all mothers. My tears continue. The image expands to connecting with the universal fear of death and loss. Can my spirituality offer me solace in the face of this? Isn't loss one of the primary facts that draws us to a spiritual path? I think about how angry I get when I hear pat answers to the question, "Why?" Don't tell me about karma, or God's Will, or that it's part of a lesson. Those answers bypass the sorrow, my experience of grief. This sculpture before me honors this. Somehow that look of innocence is even more compelling than if Mary's face had appeared ravaged and racked with sorrow. She needs compassion. She needs me to accompany her, be present with her. This allows me to gain strength from the shared human experience. I am not alone.

In this moment, I understand the power of the creative

moment to transcend time and space—to draw me through the act
of creation to a place of truth. Michelangelo was only twenty-five
when he created this work. What did he know? I've lived twice as
many years as he had—yet the place from which his genius and
inspiration comes is timeless and universal. It emerges from the
ground of being and includes me in it.

Art can stir many emotions and states of consciousness, but the
contemplation of beauty always seems to be accompanied by feelings
of love. Think about times when you were at a concert, or watching a
sunset, or captivated by the beauty of a campfire or the magnificence of
a newborn child. Did you not experience feelings of awe, an expansion
of openness and loving feelings? Perhaps the beautiful moment then
extended beyond the initial source of beauty, enlivening your senses and
leaving you with a loving feeling toward all things.

The world's spiritual traditions certainly recognize the power of
this path. The spiritual art of the world encompasses some of the most
inspired architecture, caligraphy, paintings, frescoes, and sculptures that
humanity has ever created. The greatest poets of higher consciousness,
including the author of the psalms, the poet John Donne, the philosopher-
poet Mevlana Rumi, Dante, and many others, can offer just the right
phrase to suddenly cause an expansion in you. The devotional music
of the world, both traditional and modern, also provides doorways to
higher consciousness. Meditative and sacred music is designed for this
very purpose, but certain secular music can also bring us to this level of
illumination. Look in the back of this book for our own very individual,
idiosyncratic list of favorite inspired musical works.

To facilitate your experience of higher consciousness through the contemplation of art, experiment with the following exercise.

Reflection on Art

1. Find an image that attracts you—such as a favorite painting or photograph.

2. Sit in a comfortable position and place the image at eye level.

3. Observe the image in as much detail as possible.

4. Notice what you are feeling as you observe this image.

5. Close your eyes and imagine the image inside you. Again, notice what feelings this evokes.

6. Now open your eyes and contemplate the image with an openness to the information it holds for you.

7. Make some notes on your experience and draw any of the images that came to you during this reflection.

By doing this, you become more aware of what is attracting you in this work of art. You can notice at a more intimate level the meaning and emotional effect it inspires in you.

If the path of the arts appeals to you, you can now make it a deliberate choice to expose yourself more often to those works that inspire you. In your home or office, become aware of the images and sounds around you, and see how you can increase the inspirational level of what you are exposed to everyday.

The Path of Service

We have trained hundreds of health professionals around the world to use imagery and meditation in their work, and they have told us many stories of having experienced illuminations during the course of their service to others in hospitals, clinics, agencies and private practices. We often feel that there is a mystical underground in the health professions (especially nurses) that is comprised of people who are drawn to service just because it opens them to moments of personal transcendence and higher consciousness. Our theory, as we have said, is that service generates illumination because it asks you to surrender your habitual patterns, which in turn frees your consciousness to have newer, subtler experiences of reality. But what, in particular, does service ask you to open to? It asks you to connect with another person, to accept him as he is, to let go of judgments in your own mind, to imagine what it must be like for the other person—in a word, to love. Every act of service, if you are consciously choosing to perform it, can open you to an expansion of love within you. You may be giving to another, but you are the one receiving: As it says in the Bible, "Give and you shall receive."

Dramatic examples of heroes on this path, such as Mother Teresa and Florence Nightingale, often inspire acts of service in the rest of us, thereby expanding the number of us taking ethical and loving actions in the world. On our journey together in this book, we saw the path of service embodied by Virgil and Beatrice as guides for the Pilgrim.

You do not need to be in a service profession to practice service as your way to higher consciousness. Being of service results from the way you treat others in any circumstance of your daily life. You can, for example, give out kindness, with amazing results, while you are simply ordering a sandwich or buying a newspaper.

Personally, we recall a powerful and inspiring act of service we received one June day when we visited a retreat center in Tuscany. We had driven deep into the countryside to find a Franciscan monastery that was now being used as a residential drug rehabilitation center.

A young man named Pietro greeted us at the gate and took us on a pre-arranged tour. He had a handsome, almost beautiful face, and a natural sweetness to his manner. Later, he told us that he generally reserves twenty minutes for a tour and was surprised that we had been talking together for four hours. These things can happen when you're standing together in a thirteenth-century grotto where St. Francis of Assisi taught his followers—you just go outside of time.

The jasmine and oleander bushes were heavy with flowers giving off powerfully sweet fragrances. Bright sunshine played through the trees and onto the buttery golden travertine of the cloister walls as Pietro told us about how the center had come into being.

In the 1960s, a visionary monk was looking for a place to hold retreats. He had become aware of more and more people who seemed directionless, lost, in crisis, and doubting themselves in some fundamental way, and he thought that this abandoned Franciscan monastery would be a place where such people could come to reflect, reconnect with their values, and find new direction for their life.

When the monk was first given permission to use it, the monastery was in a state of neglect and total deterioration. Walls had collapsed, garbage was everywhere, all the windows were broken. The monk, raised in the country and used to hard work, took on the repair work with some of the local people volunteering to help him.

Then, as Pietro put it, "the drug boom hit Italy," and heroin addiction began to reach frightening proportions. Pietro himself had been found near death from a heroin overdose in front of the Milan train station. Soon, people who had heard about the retreat center began to think of it as a place to go for help. The monk took in addicts as residents and put them to work repairing the monastery, and grateful families began to make financial contributions.

The monk never spoke about drugs to the residents. He was not interested in drug treatment. Rather, he was interested in discovering "the seed," the sublime potential in each person, and he gave the residents a chance to work at a variety of tasks in order to create the conditions for their seed, their potential, to reveal itself to them.

There were certainly many tasks to perform: preparing the ground for planting, tending the vegetable garden, harvesting, preparing meals, serving food, cleaning the kitchen, procuring additional supplies from the local farmers, repairing the paths and walls, tutoring one another, mentoring new residents, participating in dialogue with local community leaders, and, as the center flourished, running a gift shop for visitors, creating items for sale, and opening a small restaurant.

Pietro said he had found his seed by communicating honestly with people. He was listening very closely one day to what someone was telling him, and he felt the desire to speak back kindly but with absolute honesty. He could feel the relief of honest words coming out of his mouth. This simple act created for him a state of peace and comfort inside his own skin, a feeling he had not had since he was a little child. He began to seek out more situations in which communication was the task, such as accompanying the monk to meetings with the local townspeople or giving tours of the center. He began to apply this listening carefully to all interactions. He would center himself in listening to what the other person was saying and listening to his own thoughts about what he wanted to say honestly in return.

As we talked with him that day, the results of his practice were palpable in his quiet presence and the sense we had of wanting to share with him our most intimate thoughts. He seemed to be focused completely on us, as if he was speaking directly to some longing deep inside us.

Later, driving back through the countryside, we were both filled with sadness. It seemed an odd emotion to have been evoked by so inspiring an experience, and we decided to pull off the road and talk about what we were feeling so that we could better understand it. We felt that a deeper part of us, inspired by Pietro's words and the monk's accomplishments, had been activated, calling upon us to review our lives and questioning our real worth. What was our seed? What, if anything, had we done with it? Pietro had truly embodied the path of service, and he was like a mirror held up to our own path of service as health professionals, reminding us of why we were in it in the first place.

Social action is a branch of the path of service. It might, initially, seem that political activism is about as far removed from higher consciousness as one could get, but it, too, combines the liberation from focus on oneself with the conscious choice to connect to the experience of others, causing one's consciousness to become attentive to new levels of thought and feeling. Social action, of course, can take you down into the hell of rage, but it is a righteous rage concerned not with self-preservation but with reducing the suffering of others. Martin Luther King often described a higher state that transcended all fear and gave him great peace while in the middle of a social action.

If you are drawn to service or social action, you can approach it as part of your spiritual path. Dante placed a high value on social action, seeing good leadership as creating the climate for individuals to develop personally and enhance the community.

We have had several patients over the years who thought of

their social activism as the opposite of spirituality. One of them equated her activism with being realistic and practical, and viewed spirituality as the exact opposite—a kind of useless, passive fantasy. Anne described herself as being hostile to, even disgusted by, religious or spiritual leaders who comment on social problems but do nothing to change them. When we discussed her own motives for activism, she described the pain she feels in her chest whenever she sees injustice. She said she might have turned to activism just to alleviate that pain.

During one therapy session, we asked her to close her eyes and bring her attention to the area where the pain usually occurs. Then we asked her to convert the pain into a picture in her imagination. She saw a small child, poorly dressed, frightened, helpless. Her description of the child's pain was so detailed that it appeared as if her consciousness had entered completely into the child's experience. Anne's inner life was manifested in her outward behavior exactly as it would be in anyone on a path to higher consciousness—creating liberation of the self from personal fears, expanding the self into unity with others, and learning to identify one's life purpose and be true to it.

If you believe the path of service might be a way for you to experience higher consciousness, try the following exercise.

Compassion

This is an attitude of service you can practice even for a minute as you ride on a bus, sit in a public area, or wait on a line. You are "serving" not by performing any specific act but by generating an inner attitude toward others. We have had our students try this by walking around the block from our training center, and they come back reporting a heightened sense of unity with, and positive reactions from complete strangers.

1. Close your eyes just for a moment. Prepare yourself, when you open them, to look at the person across from you in the usual way we look at people—comparing them to ourselves, noting their imperfections, sizing them up as safe/unsafe, better than/less than, identifying them ethnically, economically—all those rapid-fire evaluations and opinions we come up with.

2. Open your eyes and look at the person across from you in this way…

3. Now close your eyes and notice how you feel…

4. With your eyes still closed, begin to prepare yourself to look at the person across from you as a soul like you who is briefly here to learn…

5. Open your eyes and begin to look at him with this attitude….

6. Now close your eyes and notice how you feel…

We all know that, beneath the appearance of our differences, we are in the same human situation together, and the shift of attitude in this exercise connects us to that knowing. You suddenly see others more as brothers and sisters rather than as strangers. You feel more friendliness, and it shows up on your face, in your eyes, in the way you look at others. Other people sense that and, at least sometimes, feel safe enough to reflect it back to you. Your focused awareness on this compassionate attitude also suspends the normal distractions and conflicts in your mind, resulting in more peace in your mood and body.

· ·

Thus far, we have discussed the arts and service as two paths to higher consciousness because they are readily available to virtually everyone everyday and can help "create the conditions" for illumination. A third path to follow would be to make some form of meditation and/ or prayer a part of your life.

The Path of Meditation and Prayer

When you meditate, you are purposefully directing your consciousness in a new way.

Rather than allowing it to roam all over the place, from one thought to another, to a feeling, a sensation, an urge, you are choosing to focus it on one object. You may want to refer back to the *Witnessing the Body* practice in Chapter Two as a method for focusing your consciousness. People who use this practice generally have one of three experiences: They become distracted by random thoughts and do not remain focused; they go into a trancelike state; or they remain present in the moment. If you find random thoughts intruding or discover that your mind has gone into a trance, it's important that you bring your consciousness back to the moment. Distraction and trance lead you nowhere while the practice of staying present will provide you with immediate benefits.

You will be able to focus on any activity with more ease and pleasure, and you will feel increasing periods of greater peace. Spiritually, you will begin to establish a relationship with a deeper reality in your nature—you as a living center of consciousness. That center already exists, and as you practice staying present, it will become more and more available to you.

New feelings—including a refreshed, calm wakefulness, inner peace, lightly pervading joy, subtle visions and voices, energy changes such as a pleasurable solidity, or an almost levitating lightness will become more common. What is happening is that your consciousness is being temporarily freed from the heaviness and constriction of your habitual patterns, and you are discovering a part of yourself that is already light and harmonious. You are not *creating* this harmonious state by meditating, but rather you are *discovering* it through meditation. Assagioli described this relationship with your deeper center as "something sure, permanent, and indestructible."

His own path of meditation was put to a severe test when he was arrested and imprisoned in 1940, but his notes tell very little about the fears he must have felt. Instead, they speak about the illuminative states he began to experience:

A sense of boundlessness, of no separation from all that is, a merging with… the whole. First an outward movement, but not towards any particular object or individual being—an overflowing of effusion in all directions, like an ever expanding sphere. A sense of universal love. Then the ability to focus the love towards some object or individual and at the same time to specialize its quality. A compassionate love toward the inmates of my prison and towards all prisoners and inmates of hospitals; tender love to the members of my family, a brotherly love towards my friends, a love… admiration, gratitude, [and] veneration towards the great souls of the world, the wise, and particularly toward Christ, the embodiment of love. But all of these qualifications of love always remained with the whole, the Whole of Reality, of Life. A wonderful merging. No separation— only differing aspects of wonder.

The notes continue with an inarticulate reaching for words to recapture and describe the experience:

Essential Reality is so far above all mental conceptions. It is inexpressible. It has to be lived. Joy inherent in Life Itself, in the very Substance of Reality... The realization of the Self, resting and standing in itself... The selfless Self... merged into God... the realization of our true self.

Dante reached for similar language to express his own breakthrough experience: "Light eternal, fixed in Self alone, known only to Yourself, you love and glow, knowing and being known..."

If Assagioli was unable to find words adequate to describe his experience of higher consciousness, he was, nevertheless, able to outline in his notes the path he had taken to arrive at that state. "Method: (1) Physical relaxation, rhythmic breathing. (2) Emotional quiet. Affirmation. (3) Stilling the mind. (4) Raising of consciousness to deeper levels...through radiation of love—deep conviction of the reality and effectiveness of psychospiritual radiation of compassionate love to the inmates...[to] the world..."

He completes those notes with a startling insight:

I realized that I was free to take one or another attitude toward the situation, to give one or another value to it, to utilize it or not in one way or another. I could rebel. I could submit passively, vegetating. Or I could indulge myself in the unwholesome pleasure of self-pity and assume the martyr's role. Or I could take the situation with a sense of humor, or I could make it a rest cure, or I could submit my self to psychological experiments on myself. Or finally, I could make it a spiritual retreat—at last away from the world. There was no doubt in my mind—I was responsible.

While there are many forms of meditation, our experience has been that the "raising consciousness to deeper levels" is most effectively facilitated when you engage the power of your imagination through the use of imagery for the sake of illumination. You can think of this practice as a creative meditation.

Both Roman Catholicism and Tibetan Buddhism make extensive use of art and images to awaken spiritual experiences. And this form of creative meditation was also a primary tool in Assagioli's work—so much so that many professionals equate psychosynthesis with imagery work.

Assagioli explored imagery and symbols in great depth. Drawing from folk tales, mythology, and art, as well as his own spontaneous inner images and those of his patients and students, he catalogued the universal images that were most often associated with illuminative states of experience.

Perhaps the single most familiar image of higher consciousness is the mountain, which appears throughout the world's spiritual art as the symbol of a higher view—a higher mind. Other images of higher consciousness include descent into the underworld (for example, the Pilgrim's descent into hell), going on a journey or pilgrimage, the face of someone in a state of illumination (such as the serenely smiling Buddha), the beauty of a flower, life rising out of destruction (resurrection), the emergence of radiant light, the interaction of water and light, the seasons of the year, the rising or setting of the sun, the courage of heroes, a being or deity of absolute unconditional love such as Kuan Yin (the Chinese Buddha of compassion) or Mary, and many others.

In keeping with his belief that it is necessary to create the conditions conducive to experiencing higher consciousness, Assagioli encouraged his patients and students to find images of higher consciousness among the art treasures of Florence to use in their meditation practice, and in the following chapter we will talk about the way we ourselves have used Florentine art as a means to encourage meditation.

Assagioli's appreciation of imagery is at least in part attributable to his Italian background. During the Italian Renaissance (1400-1550), a hundred years after Dante, school children were taught how to visualize themselves in the action of sacred paintings as a way to encourage their spiritual development. In fact, some Renaissance painters, such as Jacopo Pontormo, deliberately painted non-distinct faces so that the viewer could more easily imagine himself as the figure next to Jesus or the figure in contact with an angel.

Imagery Meditation

When you first try these practices, find a place where you can be relatively free of distraction. It will help to begin either by working with a friend or by making an audiotape of the instructions for yourself. It is important when following these instructions to go very slowly, allowing yourself time to notice new sensations, images, and emotions. You can practice the two meditations that follow over and over again. It would be a good idea to keep notes for yourself to see the progression of your experiences. Do not be surprised if you become distracted during imagery meditation; that is normal, as it is during all meditation. Simply return yourself to the meditation once you notice you have drifted off.

Imagery: The Rose

As only one of many possibilities, Assagioli developed a

meditation on the unfolding of a rose, which was one of his favorite images of growth and development. He pointed out that, in both Eastern and Western traditions, flowers are frequently used to represent the soul or the spiritual self. And Dante himself, as we will see, also used the rose as a symbol of illumination.

Read the instructions through and then try this exercise for yourself.

1. Close your eyes and connect with your breathing.

2. Allow your mind to focus fully on the sensation of your breath passing through your nostrils... As soon as you are aware of any other thoughts or sensations, bring your attention back to your breath.

3. Now, in your imagination, visualize a rosebush... Notice it in as much detail as possible.

4. Now become aware of a tightly closed bud on one of the branches... Focus on this bud... Now imagine the force of life gently moving into it and opening it.

5. Now identify with this life energy blossoming and opening in you at the same time... Stay with this experience as long as it lasts...

Imagery: Visualization Meditation

Select an image that you feel drawn to for this meditation. It can be overtly spiritual, such as a religious figure, or a personal hero of yours, or any other image that inspires you and suggests a depth of quality or beauty you want to explore. Place the image you have chosen at eye level in front of you.

1. Make your body comfortable...

2. Let the chair hold you...

3. Now follow your breathing...

4. Now let your breathing breathe on its own and just witness it...

5. Now look at the image. Explore what it means to you.

6. Now close your eyes and follow your breathing.

7. When you feel centered, open your eyes and gaze softly at the image... Notice what part of it you are drawn to... and then begin to bring that part of it inside, into your imagination, as you close your eyes.

8. Follow the inward effect of the image, whether it is visual, emotional, or mental.

9. And now, in your imagination, become that image... Identify with it and see the world from its perspective... What is your experience? What do you feel? What is your view of life?

It is not necessary for these imagery exercises to be pictures in your mind. Some of us are very visual in our imagination, while for others the imagination is more easily engaged through words or feelings or combinations of sensory experience. For example, in the imagery meditation on the rose, you can imagine a rose opening without seeing it: You can imagine feeling it open, or think about it blossoming and still attain the same inner focus as the visual person. You will learn about your own style of imagination as you practice these exercises.

The power and beauty of your imagination is that it can bring creation to anything—any word, any image, any impulse. In fact, your imagination is your personal experience of the creation that is ceaselessly taking place in the world. Used properly, it can take you into new knowledge and new feelings of higher consciousness.

Illumination Through Energy Meditation

Another effective form of meditation is to focus on the energy of your body. We ourselves saw how powerful this form of meditation could be through the illumination of a student named Eileen who came to our morning meditation class to reduce her anxiety, which was based on the cold reality that she had a debilitating and life threatening illness. She was not sure meditation would be useful, but she kept coming to class to give it every chance she could. After four months, she had a breakthrough.

She was in class meditating on the energy in her hands when suddenly she began to experience her whole body as an energy field. Then she felt her awareness expanding to experience the whole meditation classroom as an energy field.

Eileen's awareness kept expanding and expanding until it took in the whole city, then the land and water surrounding the city, and finally the whole planet. Eileen experienced the whole planet as energy with her awareness distributed everywhere throughout the energy field. She could see in every direction and she was pervaded with a dancing joy. Time was gone. Confinement in the body was gone. Eileen, as she had previously defined Eileen, was gone.

When Eileen re-emerged into awareness of the meditation class a few seconds later her feeling of joy took in the entire the room and all people in it. All the colors were vibrant masterpieces, all the objects perfect. She was experiencing the aftermath of her higher state, floating on a sea of gratitude. Everything was holy.

The class ended and Eileen started toward home. As she walked, she sensed she had just been changed forever. Over the next few days, the changes kept coming to her, like ocean waves to the shore.

She no longer felt afraid of death. She now felt curious about it. But, at the same time, she also loved life more than she had before the breakthrough and was in no hurry to die.

Her mind had a new clarity and peace. She could pay deeper attention to her work, her friends, and her emotions. She could see more objectively. She could see other people's viewpoints completely and felt no attachment to arguing with them because she found it much more satisfying to whole-heartedly experience and understand their view. And she found that because she was communicating her understanding, people easily let go of their view to ask about hers. This new way of being became so noticeable at work that her boss began to ask her to handle negotiations with difficult clients.

Eileen could walk down a street and unexpectedly be in bliss at all of the richness and variety of life. Her understanding of God went from what had been for her a non-credible humanoid male super-being in the sky to a limitless interpenetrating spirit of love and order that was present here and now. This new understanding simply showed up in her mind one day without conscious effort, and each time she recalled it, she went into a deeply pleasurable state of gratitude.

Energy Meditation

Here are two energy meditations you can experiment with yourself to see if either of them is comfortable for you.

Energy Meditation on the Hands

1. Stand comfortably or sit in a straight chair.

2. Gently shake your hands for a minute...

3. Now place you hands in front of you as if you were holding a balloon, elbows at your sides, shoulders relaxed, your palms about twelve inches apart and facing each other ... Keep your hands and fingers soft and relaxed as you do this...

4. Place your awareness into the space between the palms of your hands...

5. Very slowly, begin to experiment with slowly moving your palms closer or farther apart, but always keeping the palms facing each other...

6. Keep your awareness in this space, studying the sensations between the hands...

You may experience the space between your hands as a bringing together of magnets from opposing poles and feel a slight resistance if you try to move them towards each other. Some people describe the feeling as bounciness or as aliveness. Your hands may tingle or even feel slightly charged, or your experience may be dominated by subtle pulsations in your fingertips and palms. However, you need not feel any of these sensations in order for the meditation to be effective. What you are doing is focusing on a subtle level of energy that can lead to illumination.

Energy Meditation: Sitting

1. Use a straight chair with a good back.

2. Sit close to the edge of your chair holding your back in a straight but not stiff posture ... tilt your chin down slightly, straightening the back of your neck ... keep your knees at shoulder width ... your tongue resting lightly on the roof of your mouth ... rest your hands on your legs. Relax into the posture, letting go of any tightness or stiffness ...

3. And now let your mind go easily into meditation, bringing awareness to your body ... (Do this for two minutes).

4. And now slide back into your chair, relax, and notice how you are feeling ... Do this for a minute).

5. One more time—slide forward to the edge of your chair and repeat the steps of the meditation.

You may find this posture uncomfortable at first. After two or three tries, however, it may turn out to be your favorite meditation because of its potential for allowing you to become aware of yourself as a living, dynamic energy field. Once your awareness enters your energy field, you discover that you are much more than a musculo-skeletal physical self. You are also an energy self existing in direct relationship to the energy of the universe. This is not a metaphor. It is fact.

The River of Light

Dante knew about these expansions of consciousness into the energy field, and he has the Pilgrim describe the experience for us:

The power of new sight lit up my eyes
so that no light, however bright it were,
would be too brilliant for my eyes to bear...

And I saw light that was a flowing stream...
Out of this stream the sparks of living light
were shooting up and settling on the flowers:
they looked like rubies set in rings of gold;

then as if all that fragrance made them drunk,
they poured back into that miraculous flood.

Beatrice, reading his mind, knows that he is straining to understand what he is seeing, and she tells him that both the living light (life energy) and the form it is taking (the flowers) are only intimations of the truth. She is pointing to the fact that life energy and the various forms it takes are "only" the visible results of the non-visible process of creation.

Following his teacher's advice, the Pilgrim then plunges his face into the river, immersing himself in the energy field exactly as Eileen did during her energy meditation. With the Pilgrim's eyes now filled with that energy, he sees the river transformed into a vast circle of light:

And then, as people at a masquerade
take off the masks which have until that time

been hiding their true selves -- so, then and there, ...
I saw heaven in ... reality ...

...

God ... grant me now the power to find the words for what I saw!
There is a light ... whose glory makes Creator ...
[visible to the created mind],
whose only peace is in beholding Him.

The Importance of Surrender

We are reminded again how important the concept of surrender is to illumination. The Pilgrim surrenders his doubts to his teacher's guidance and plunges his face into the river of light with the faith not only that he will be safe but also that something important awaits him.

His experience of illumination is deepening. The glorious light becomes a vast white rose containing thousands of tiers and thousands of beings with "love-dedicated faces," its petals reaching infinitely into space. This white rose, this Dantean vision of the vast ocean of being, is a symbol of the state of enlightenment.

Flowers of various kinds—including the "golden flower" in Chinese imagery, the lotus in Tibet and India, and the rose in Europe and Persia—have been used to represent the blossoming, the opening of higher states of being in both Western and Eastern spiritual traditions. Assagioli very consciously chose to use the rose in imagery meditation because of its universal symbolic value and the parallel between the unfolding of a plant and what happens within us when our "seed" of higher potential opens and blossoms.

Our Pilgrim is entranced by the magnificence of the white rose and the saintly presences before him. He is eager to understand even more, but when he turns to speak to Beatrice, he is surprised to find her gone and an old man standing in her place. When the Pilgrim asks what has happened to her, the old man replies, "I was urged by Beatrice to leave my place and end all your desire…"

The figure is St. Bernard of Clairvaux, a mystic monk known to have had a strong devotion to Mary. When the Pilgrim again inquires about Beatrice, the monk points up to the white rose, saying that she has returned to her place among the other blessed and saintly souls.

He then goes on to explain that he has been sent by Mary to guide the Pilgrim to his final destination, and that the time has come for pure contemplation. The Pilgrim is being directed to let go of his wisdom mind, his Beatrice, completely and enter into states of pure awareness, which are always the end goal of any spiritual practice. As the Pilgrim focuses his powers of contemplation on the inner light, he suddenly goes beyond all thought, all images, and feels his will and his desire being moved "by the Love that moves the sun and the other stars."

The Enduring Benefit of Higher Consciousness

After the initial fascination with illuminative experiences and their momentary joys have faded, one benefit remains forever: Higher states of consciousness renew our relationship to our natural love of life.

We can easily become disconnected from that love—whether through the fear-based patterns cataloged in hell and purgatory or simply as a result of the many sufferings we endure in our lives. To manage all this suffering, we develop defenses that are both necessary and effective. Unfortunately, however, our defenses also become habitual ways of guarding against loving and trusting. They become our armor, and our armor weighs us down. It is this armor that prevents many people from experiencing love in their lives.

The study of higher consciousness begins to lift that weight. For a few moments, an illumination raises our love up to the surface of our personality again, and we get a glimpse of the powerhouse of love that is in reserve inside us. That love then spreads its effect, letting us see the essential joy that pervades deeper reality. We see again, as Eileen did, the inherent divinity and unity in the world. We relax into the amazing fact of the world just as it is, and our being becomes light.

And, as it did for Eileen, higher consciousness also changes our relationship to death. Instinctively, we as human beings love life so much that death appears to be our enemy. It is certainly our enemy when it takes loved ones away from us forever. Higher consciousness, however, helps us make a great cognitive leap to the understanding that our human situation is not life versus death. The opposite of life is not death. There is no opposite of life. It is eternal, harmonious, exquisitely ordered, and contains all things, including death. A moment of higher consciousness allows us to taste the eternal nature of reality and to experience "the peace that surpasses all understanding."

We have spent intense weeks in Florence with groups of people looking for this peace and love, and we ask that, in the following pages, you join us on one of these journeys.

CHAPTER NINE

The Candle For Its Flame
Prepared

The Love that calms...
forever greets all those who enter...
so is the candle for Its Flame prepared.

-----Beatrice
I know I saw the universal form,
the fusion of all things, for I can feel,
while speaking now, my heart leap in joy.

-----The Pilgrim

Dante taught that love—its presence, its absence, its distortions—is the single cause of all of the joys and sorrows of humanity. Rumi taught that the end goal of all spirituality is love without an object. Assagioli referred to the "supreme heartbeat of unity" that reconciles our conflicts. And many other teachers and traditions have also found their way to this same conclusion: Love is the unifying force in the universe.

Love and unity will always be your answer. Your problems will always be some form of separation from that answer. This understanding clarifies what matters in your life and what your real problems are.

In certain breakthrough moments, when your consciousness enters and disappears into the energy field of love, you will know what the mystics of the world have always been trying to tell us, as well as what Dante meant when he described his experience of merging with "the Love that moves the sun and the other stars."

Over the years, we have had the pleasure of working with many patients and students who had decided to look for more enduring love in their life and who knew intuitively that their search would have to include more spirituality. At one point, a group of them— knowing of our attachment to Florence through Assagioli and Dante, and knowing that it is one of those places on earth that create the conditions for a breakthrough experience of spirituality—encouraged us to guide them there.

A few months later, we were in the Florence airport drinking our third cup of cappuccino and nervously awaiting the arrival of our tour group's plane. While a few of our students were coming, we were also expecting a number of complete strangers who had learned about our work and the upcoming tour. They had flown to Rome from many different cities—Los Angeles, San Francisco, Chicago, and New York— to catch their connecting flight to Florence. Finally, we saw the Air Meridiana plane appearing two hours late in the blue Tuscan sky.

When it landed, we could immediately pick out the members of our group. While the other passengers hurried to claim their baggage or to take a taxi to their final destination, our people were wandering around Florence's small airport waiting to be found.

We called out to a few, " Sacred Art tour…?" And, as they responded, others joined the gathering. We called off the names on our list and found that one woman from Los Angeles was missing. We went looking around the airport for an obvious American, spotted her in the cafeteria, and asked her to join us. She said she would after another cigarette. She had not been allowed to smoke on the plane, and she needed a few cigarettes to feel normal.

As we returned to the group, we saw that they were a very unhappy bunch of people. They had all had long flights from America to Rome, and then a short bumpy flight to Florence. Some were angry because they had endured long layovers in Rome, while others were angry because their flights had been delayed in America and they had barely made their connection to Florence. Several wanted to call and complain to the American tour company before we had even left the airport. The Sacred Art tour could wait.

We tried to raise our consciousness above it all, but a part of us was dreading the thought of spending nine days with these people. We gave them the good news that a very pleasant tour bus was waiting for them outside as soon as they got their luggage, and when the courteous driver actually came in to help the older people with their bags, some of the group actually started to smile just a little.

The bus was very pleasant but it was also too long. It had been rented through an American company in San Francisco whose personnel had obviously never seen the narrow roads bordered by stone walls north of Florence. A half-mile from the Renaissance villa where the tour group would stay, the bus made a turn into a one-lane road and got jammed against the wall, unable to move either forward or back. It was a beautiful but very hot day, and we all sat there sweating as we tried to figure out what to do.

Luckily, we didn't have to decide. A priest who was visiting the villa had been headed back to Florence on the road we were now blocking. He got out of his car, spoke with our driver, and then, immediately and cheerfully, offered to start driving our people up to the villa. His car held only three at a time, one of whom was crammed into a tiny back seat. After his first trip, however, he recruited a nun from the villa and returned with her driving a second car. In the midst of this operation, two policemen arrived. At first they seemed indignant at having to deal with this screwy situation. Then, however, they went about their business, blocking off traffic to the south of us so that the bus could back out of the lane—an operation that could not be accomplished without much scraping of the bus against the stone walls and much angry dialogue between police and driver, the essence of which seemed to be that driver thought the police were crazy for telling him to ruin the bus, and the police were telling the driver that he would be in even more trouble if he stayed there blocking the lane.

Waiting for the priest and the nun to pick up more people, we watched the poor bus driver grimacing painfully as he heard the sides of his bus scraping and scratching. When the bus was finally free, he backed it further into a restaurant parking lot, and the two of us began to unload the luggage, which the priest and the nun would then deliver to the villa. Finally, four hours later than we had planned, we arrived exhausted at the villa with the last piece of luggage.

Although we were anxious about what the group's reaction to the bus incident might be, the humor of the situation, and perhaps their jet lag, seemed to have loosened them up. By the time we sat down to a delicious dinner cooked by the nuns, everyone was sweet and mellow. The pasta was tasty, the vegetables fresh, and the Chianti was very popular. We all began to feel the quiet sense of camaraderie that develops in people and animals when they have had a lot to eat.

After dinner, the mother superior proudly showed us to the espresso machine that stood prominently in the entrance hallway. For a thousand lire (about fifty cents), the machine ground a portion of fresh black beans and then went on to produce a single shot of rich espresso. One man from Los Angeles was so impressed that he vowed to get one for his office.

Espressos in hand, we gathered briefly in the library to distribute schedules for the tour. As part of our introduction, we asked each member of the group to tell the others why he or she had joined us. Every one of their answers included some statement about the magical attraction of Florence—a place they had always known they would have to visit one day. When we asked them to be more specific about the nature of their attraction, one woman said that Florence felt like the place where an important spiritual breakthrough experience could happen, and everyone agreed that a breakthrough would be exactly what they were hoping for on this journey.

It's a curious state to be in—waiting for a breakthrough. Are we in this position because our life desperately needs to change or because we already have a vague sense that something new is about to happen to us? It is confusing because we do not even know what we mean. A breakthrough to what? We do not know, but the feeling is clear. The feeling is one of longing. Longing motivates the search for the breakthrough, and longing creates the condition of willingness for something new to happen.

We were beginning to get a sense of who the people in this group really were and what they were here to do. They were more than just attracted to Florence. Certainly they were looking for new experiences, but they were also hinting at a deeper hope, one that is embarrassing to admit even in front of friends. They had not responded to the usual slick ad for a tour promising five cities in seven days riding in an air-conditioned bus with big suppers and lots of drinks at the end of each day. This group had come to Florence to learn how to meditate on sacred art. They were a group of people seeking something more. Perhaps they were responding to an intuition that this journey would guide them to have a spiritual experience.

It is touching when seekers find one another. It opens up the possibility of talking about intimate feelings of longing and the hope that they will suddenly have a clarifying vision of reality that they can believe in and trust. It is this kind of knowing that Dante meant when he wrote: "I see that each mind cannot be satisfied until it is illumined by that truth beyond which there is no other truth."

The deeper search is to know if God is truly real. God floats in the minds of millions of people as a concept that is subject to thousands of interpretations. But the seeker is not satisfied. The seeker does not want concepts, does not want interpretations. The seeker wants to know God directly. If a seeker finds out that God is real, everything is all right and the world can be trusted. If God is real, the world, as sad and as cruel as it can get, is still safe at the core because it is God's world. Then even at the time of death, life can be trusted and we can surrender to death. It is the possibility of this elemental reassurance that drives the seeker.

The first full morning of our tour gave a hint of what was to come. Bright and early, we took our group to the San Marco Museum in the Piazza San Marco. The museum is housed in a former monastery where Fra Angelico or one of his assistants had painted a fresco depicting a scene from Jesus' life on the wall of each monk's cell. We wanted to be the first ones there so that the members of our group could walk into these cells undisturbed by other visitors and have a direct, private experience of the place.

Fra Angelico, who lived from about 1400 to 1455, was one of the finest mystical artists of the early Italian Renaissance, and his work was in demand throughout Florence. He painted not the kind of light that has its source in the sun but the kind that illuminates mystical union. As one example, his *Coronation of the Virgin*, which depicts the moment of the Virgin Mary's death and reunion with her son, Jesus, in the afterlife, glows with a golden light that seems to shine from the canvas.

On our first morning, we had instructed the group to not just look at the paintings, but to meditate on them. This is the kind of visualization meditation we described in the previous chapter during which one closes one's eyes and imagines becoming one of the figures depicted in the scene. If, for example, you are looking at an image of Jesus rising from the grave, you then inwardly imagine *being* Jesus rising from the grave.

Although Westerners outside the Roman Catholic tradition may find it difficult to understand such inner practice, young Catholics are trained through the visualization of sacred images and prayer to enter into inner dialogue with higher states of consciousness. It is a way to make the idea of higher states (for example, the consciousness of a saint) and of communicating with that saint, acceptable and comfortable to the Catholic imagination, which can then lead to the opening of mystical doors in adulthood when the person may have enough experience of society to see through it and want to find a more enduring truth.

The rational mind cannot figure life out, and our instinctual mind never goes beyond its obsession with survival and safety. To discover that deeper, more enduring truth, we need to go to other levels of the mind. These other levels (for example, the wisdom mind) do factually exist, and we need a way to directly experience them.

Meditation on sacred images is one proven way to arrive at that experience. Through visualizing these sacred images inside us, we suddenly create an opening for new thoughts, new perspectives, new feelings to come to us.

The members of our tour group had wandered up and down the halls of the museum, going in and out of the various cells, noticing which images attracted them. Their assignment was to select a few images to buy prints of in the gift shop. Later that evening, we would practice visualization with the images they had chosen.

The group eventually gathered at the end of the hallway, eagerly whispering to each other about their experiences and ready to go on to another part of the museum where more of Fra Angelico's beautiful work awaited their viewing. One of the women, nervous that her husband had not yet rejoined us, went to look for him but returned a few minutes later alone.

We told her we would find him. We knew that a few of the cells had even smaller rooms attached to them and guessed he would be in one of them. He was not in any of those places. Nor was he in the restroom. Then, walking past each of the cells one more time, we saw a pair of feet sticking out from behind a half-closed door. He was sitting on the floor, his back against the wall, with a sad sweet smile on his face. He was big guy, a former college football player, but now older, tired, wiser, with eyes that said he had experienced losses in his life. He was sitting on the floor so that he could look directly into the eyes of St. Dominic, who, in the painting at which he was staring, was sitting on the ground directly underneath Jesus on the cross. We went back to the group and told the man's wife that he was fine, but not to hurry him.

When he rejoined us, he gave his wife a hug and said he would talk to her later. The group was courteous enough to let him have his privacy, but several people kept glancing at him, trying to guess what had happened. Something was in the air for the group, and we had just started together.

The next day, we slowed the pace. We got up late and went to a country restaurant in Cercina where the staff brought out dish after dish of delicious fresh food. On our way back to Florence, a few people spotted a little hilltop church and wanted to stop. The bus driver drove us up there and then headed for the shade of a big tree. He was a courteous man and never gave the slightest hint of his reactions to the crazy Americans who wanted to go into a small country church on a hot

Sunday afternoon.

The sunlight was blazing in a sapphire blue sky. In the fertile valley below stood row upon row of olive trees with silvery green leaves and thick ancient trunks, and, two more valleys away, we could see the red-tiled roofs of Florence.

Inside, the church was dark, with the smell of incense from the morning mass still in the air. Votive candles were flickering in one of the side chapels, and the atmosphere was quietly peaceful. As we walked around, we found a poem taped to one of the columns. Our dear Florentine friend and colleague, Susie, translated it for us:

> We are surrounded by noise,
> by confusion, by words.
> But life needs peacefulness, too.
> In the silence of your heart
> as it prays or weeps, fears or hopes,
> you can find a light to illuminate you.
> You can see so much better, you can meet the Divine.
> Silence has God for a friend,
> in which you can grasp mystery.
> Pure knowledge takes form.
> You can distinguish His delicate scent.
> Never before has there been
> such a need for those who love silence.
> At times, just a little silence is all it takes
> to learn to love life again.

We saw an open door leading to an inner cloister and quietly suggested to the group that they take a look. Following the last of them through the door, we came upon a startling scene. The group was standing against the walls in semi-darkness, staring at the open center where, in blinding white sunlight there sat, on a white chair, a nun dressed completely in white, knitting a white sweater. We kept looking to make sure the nun was a real person and not an illusion. We guessed the group was doing the same.

Suddenly, the nun stood up, and the group moved toward her as if on signal. She began to speak in Italian, and Susie translated the nun's words for us: "Sometimes we have to stop looking down and we have to look up like little children," she said.

We waited for more, but there was no more, and the nun sat down again. She looked at her knitting for a while, and then resumed her work. Several members of the group began to cry, and others looked away, hiding their feelings. Then, one by one, they began to find their way back to the bus, where conversation was instantly intense and filled with questions about the nature of what we had just seen and felt together. We had all suddenly become the Pilgrim, wanting an explanation for an experience we had not even absorbed yet.

That evening, we presented a brief discussion on Renaissance art, focusing on how innovative it was of the artists of that time to depict the religious figures in sacred paintings as real human beings. Previously, these figures had been remote, idealized, otherworldly images. The artists of the Renaissance, however, wanted to engage the viewer in the depicted events by painting figures showing emotions with which the viewer could identify so that he would understand spirituality and spiritual feeling as taking place in the world, as an aspect of living, human expression rather than something that was relegated only to the afterlife. For this reason, Annunciations, Nativities and other classic depictions of the Christian story were set in familiar Florentine

"… Sometimes we have to stop looking down and we have to look up like little children…"

and Tuscan street scenes and landscapes with characters in the scenes depicting familiar faces, portraits of local people. Dante's revolutionary and insightful description of an average human being journeying on a path to illumination had deeply influenced this transformation in thinking.

In our discussion that evening, we focused on Annunciation paintings, which depict the angel Gabriel announcing to the Virgin Mary that she will become pregnant and bring Jesus into the world. Different artists have shown Mary responding in various ways to this news. She is, after all, a young woman who has just had a life-changing experience.

In some paintings, such as Botticelli's *Annunciation,* which hangs in the Uffizi Gallery in Florence, she is shown as turning away from and rejecting Gabriel. In others she is shown with one hand in the air, as if asking a question, while her other hand rests on a book. This pose, commonly referred to as the "inquiry posture," is intended to indicate that she needs more information. A lot, after all, is being asked of her.

Still other artists have depicted her with her hands folded in submission or standing alone, looking directly out of the canvas, with her hands in a gesture of benediction (a blessing) intended for the viewer.

As Ruth, a member of our group, looked at the various slides she felt drawn to the rejecting Mary of Botticelli. Ruth, like the majority of the travelers in our group, was not Catholic and had never before spent much time looking at this kind of imagery. She had always just thought of it simply as "famous art."

Spiritually, Ruth described herself as having been raised with "American social religion," meaning that you went to church on Sunday just as you went to work on Monday. You did it because you are supposed to, because you were a "good" person, and because everyone else was doing it. You did not expect much from church except the unstated self-satisfaction that derived from having done a "good thing." The minister's sermons were usually "nice," the other people in the church were "nice," and that was how you tried to keep it. You did not speak about disturbing subjects. You did not ask challenging questions. You dressed well, and you were on your best behavior. You might daydream but you pretended to be interested, and you were glad when it was over so that you could go home and change into more comfortable clothes.

Here was Ruth in Catholic Italy where dead saints' tongues are on display. Splinters of wood from the Cross, shreds of Christ's shroud, bits of nine hundred-year-old fingers and leg bones are enshrined in exquisitely crafted gold and silver, jewel-encrusted reliquaries, bejeweled containers containing relics of saints and the cross. Paintings of Jesus dripping with blood and saints being martyred hang on the walls. Incense and votive candles are burning everywhere, and people are praying lovingly to paintings of Mary holding her dead son in her arms or to paintings of Jesus holding his own beating heart in his hand. Ruth had heard about Catholics but she had never seen any of this close up. The intellectual part of her was looking at it as a kind of anthropology course—a visit to a strange, exotic culture.

She remembered a friend having told her that, "Catholics worship statues." Ruth had never seen that growing up. There were no Catholic churches in her Midwestern town. Now she thought she was seeing it. She repeated the remark to Liz, another member of the group, who later came up to us and said, "Ruth thinks we worship statues."

Knowing this, we were curious to see her buying many prints of images of Mary in the Santa Croce church gift shop the following afternoon. Mary is mentioned and honored in the Koran of Islam far more than she is by American Protestants, who do not elevate her in the way that Catholics do.

That evening we gathered in the small library of the villa to practice visualization meditation. (See the Visualization Meditation exercise in Chapter Eight.) Ruth found a private corner of the library, set her chosen image, which was the rejecting Mary of Botticelli's *Annunciation*, at eye level, closed her eyes, and prepared to center her body through quiet focus on her breath. When she felt ready, she would open her eyes and gaze softly at the image. Then, again when she was ready, she would close her eyes and imagine being the image.

As Ruth turned her attention to her breath, it seemed anxious, hurried. "Calm down," she said to herself, and soon her breath became subtler, quieter. When a feeling of soothing relaxation came over her, she opened her eyes and gazed at Mary. She saw Mary's concerned face, her body twisted away from the angel, her rejecting hand. Ruth looked and looked, but felt nothing.

Disappointed, she closed her eyes and, suddenly, images and memories began to come to her. At first, she did not realize how they were connected to one another. Then it became clear—they were all impulses and fantasies of running away, of being far away from everything, of being off wandering in the hills, of leaving the world and living like a hermit, of living alone by the sea instead of in the habitual conformity of her town. She had always felt this longing, and she had always turned away from it, putting her attention on the surface of life, being good, being nice, and, above all, being like everyone else. The pull of that longing had always been so vague and hidden and subtle, while the demands of husband, children, teaching, and social obligations had always been spelled-out and obvious.

She was 64 years old now and retired. She had never before traveled alone, but her husband had no interest in this trip. She had never acted on her longing before. She was not young. She did not have all the time in the world. What was she waiting for? Why had she not said "yes" to her inner feelings sooner? What was she afraid of? Would she ever say "yes?" What would make her do it? Someone's death? And what would she do? Would she divorce her husband? He was a good man. They had had a good life. Why would she leave him now? But if she did not leave him, if she did not change her life, how would she act on her feeling? She did not know.

She wondered why all these questions were running through her mind. Where were they coming from? Ruth snapped out of her reflection and looked again at the image of Mary. She felt close to Mary in a way she could not have imagined ten minutes earlier. There was no rational basis for the closeness but it felt absolutely true. She whispered to the Mary image, "I understand." And she felt a strange thrill saying those words, as if she had opened a door to something unknown.

When Ruth emerged from her corner of the library, she smiled at everyone, waved to us, and walked out into the starry night. The white wisteria covering the entrance to the villa and the tall lavender and rosemary bushes lining the path filled the air with sweetness and spice. Ruth looked at the lights of Florence down below and listened to dogs barking in the distant darkness. It was cool out, but Ruth felt a rising heat in her belly that then began to radiate throughout her torso and face. Her feet were solidly on the ground, but her head felt like it was opening, like the walls of her skull were dropping away to make room for the wave of being that was moving through her. She disappeared into the feeling for a long time, and then was back again in the cool night, pervaded by joy. She was feeling what the Pilgrim felt when he exclaimed, "I seemed to see all of the universe turn into a smile…Joy! Ecstasy!…Life complete…!"

Yet another member of our group, Christina, knew by the time she began her medical studies that she wanted to leave Poland. She studied English as much as she studied medicine, and by the age of 23, she was writing letters to the administrators of postgraduate medical programs in the United States. Her ambition to go to America was alternately encouraged by her family and used against her as a source of guilt. She became known as "the American."

Christina could see beyond her cultural conditioning. She could feel her inner promise, and she knew that there was something for her out there in the bigger world. Deep into the night, when others were sleeping, Christina would be actively thinking up new ideas. She considered her mind to be her personal treasure, and sometimes, in the night, she lay in bed thanking her mind and telling her mind that she loved it.

She valued science, where the mind could study anything, and she hated religion, where the mind was allowed only certain thoughts. She viewed her religion, Catholicism, as a rich corporation selling fantasy, and the hypocrisy of the local priest drove her crazy with frustration. People like Christina, who react so violently against religion, are usually deep spiritual seekers in disguise. Spirituality means so much to them that they are enraged by any violation of its intention.

Why had Christina come to Florence? The group as a whole had revealed itself to be made up of God-seekers with Christina the angry exception. For the first few days she almost snarled at the sacred art in the museums we visited, and one day we actually overheard her telling her husband, "One more crucifix and I'm going to vomit."

When the nuns served dinner, Christina was often impolite, commenting out loud in English that all the meals had meat, implying that the nuns were backward and insensitive. She was an intensely self-righteous vegetarian, often going on and on about it as we walked the streets or sat at a coffee bar. Her husband would sheepishly smile in agreement, but his nostrils flared with pleasure when a meat dish went past him.

The meals the nuns served were plain and hearty, usually pasta with some meat or chicken flavorings, and vegetables from the villa's garden. Each evening, Christina would stare at the first course brought out from the kitchen, examining it for any violation of her strict vegetarianism. The rest of us would wait for her to pass judgment and then go on to eat our pasta or soup with great appreciation. Christina, who had been a person apart in her Polish culture, had now made herself a person apart in our own little temporary culture of tourists around a table in the hills north of Florence.

She was clearly angry with us as tour leaders for what she saw as our hypocrisy. Here we were, claiming to be leading a Sacred Art tour, and yet eating cooked animal flesh without the slightest hesitation. Christina had a strong sense of injustice for any insensitivity except the kind she imposed on the rest of us.

Whenever we went into the city, she seemed undecided about whether or not to stay with the group. She would often take her husband aside to whisper in his ear, and then she would send him over to tell us they were going off by themselves and would see us at 6 P.M. in the Piazza della Repubblica, our designated meeting place. She was struggling with the Catholic images, she was struggling with the food, she was struggling with us, and she was struggling with being part of the group.

Her transformation began on our fourth night. Gathered in the villa library after dinner, we explained that, by the time of the Italian Renaissance, the leading scholars were embracing the writings of the pre-Christian Greek and Roman philosophers and envisioning a universal religion based on humanistic values. Many of the Greek works had been preserved and translated by Islamic scholars and were, therefore, available only in Arabic. Renaissance patrons, however, had funded and supported the search for and translation of these texts, and, as a result, the Italian Renaissance scholars were now able to discern the common thread at the heart of all religions. As we talked, we noticed that this information seemed to be appealing to Christina, probably because it gave such value to the mind.

We then went on to discuss the influence of *The Divine Comedy* on the development of Italian Renaissance humanism. One outstanding characteristic of Dante's Pilgrim is his rage at the hypocrisy of the church, which, he felt, should have been one of the great stabilizing and humanizing forces in the world. In addition, the idea that Dante's love of a woman might be the driving force for spiritual illumination was anathema at a time when the official dogma was that all love had to be focused on God and any object that drew a person's spiritual attention away from love of God was sinful. In addition to which, women were still seen as evil because of the role Eve had played in the fall from paradise. The popular force of Dante's poem startled the culture of his time. It was studied, memorized, and even chanted aloud in the streets of Florence.

Hearing all this, Christina looked at us warmly and leaned forward in her chair. What we had to say next drew her in even more. We explained that for us, the beauty of Dante as a spiritual sage is that he never abandoned his personality. He allowed himself the honesty of his emotional reactions and never once suggested that spirituality meant having to abandon or suppress our individuality.

By this time we had Christina's full attention. The seeker in her, repressed for so many years by her anger and cynicism, was hearing a welcoming wake-up call. The next night, we were intrigued to see that she had brought prints of sacred images to our evening visualization practice. Previously, she had not even bothered to show up.

Without asking for help, Christina prepared for visualization. She found a very private corner of the library and taped up a print of Fra Angelico's *The Virgin and Child Enthroned with St. John the Baptist and St. Mark* (the centerpiece of the monumental Linaiuoli triptych in the San Marco Museum.) Adjusting her chair to just the right distance from the image, she took a few long breaths and then settled herself down to gaze at it.

Her first reaction was one of great doubt. What did the painting actually depict? She first saw Mary as subdued, sad, even depressed. The Church might present this scene as sacred, but Christina saw in the artist's intention the display of a trapped young woman playing out her fate. Then, realizing that she might be projecting her own feelings onto Mary, she closed her eyes in order to start over.

She looked at Mary for a second time. Now she saw a pretty young woman caught up in a monumental drama. Christina had listened to enough of what we'd been saying to understand that the red cross on the baby Jesus' halo symbolized his having come into this world as an enlightened being with a knowledge of victory over death. She began to realize that the young Mary was holding a child who was going to die before her and to sense the bravery of her having accepted that condition of her baby's birth. Mary had to love what she knew she would lose. Suddenly, Christina understood that this was why she herself had never wanted children. She had always sensed that she had only a limited capacity to love, and even so she imagined she would go crazy if she ever lost her child.

Images of mothers began to flood Christina's mind. The images all spoke to the difficult conditions and fears and personal restrictions mothers must overcome in order to love fully. Christina closed her eyes again with the understanding that she was learning more and more from looking at Mary. That understanding appealed tremendously to her love of the mind and of knowledge, and she felt more openness and excitement about preparing to look at Mary for a third time. She was becoming a candle prepared for its flame.

Beatrice is teaching the Pilgrim about this kind of preparation when she says, "The Love that calms…forever greets all those who enter…so is the candle for Its Flame prepared," and her words trigger in him the following experience:

No sooner had these brief, assuring words entered my ears
than I was fully aware my senses were now raised beyond their powers;
The power of new sight lit up my eyes so that no light,
no matter how bright, would be too brilliant for my eyes to bear.

Christina opened her eyes and gazed softly at Mary. She felt a thrill pass through her, and suddenly she was riveted by Mary's eyes. Great compassion seemed to be flowing from those eyes. Everything tense, everything guarded about Christina was gone. She felt she was in direct contact with Mary's bravery and her profoundly serene state of consciousness, and feeling that bravery caused a soaring sensation within her, the sensation of being pulled up.

The suddenness and power of that upward pull became frightening, and she grabbed onto her chair, terrified that she would be smashed into the ceiling. But it was hopeless. The force was too powerful. Christina gave in, surrendered. And as soon as she did, her fear was gone.

She felt a rapid rise upward. Suddenly, she was traveling at high speed through a tunnel. She felt supremely peaceful.

She entered into brilliant white light and felt her cellular structure merging into the light. She was disappearing and the intensity of that feeling was indescribably blissful. She instantaneously understood that she had discovered not only her own but everyone's true home.

Dante describes the same experience this way:

There is a light whose glory
makes the Creator visible to the created mind...

Christina was overwhelmed with the joy knowing she was home. And then, for a while, she was gone into bliss as the only awareness, with no self left to notice or describe. She had ended.

The next thing she knew, she was observing the slow formation of an image in her mind. The image became an old woman crying tears of salt. The salt, running down the woman's face for years and years, had cut deep grooves like river gorges in her skin. Christina's instantaneous understanding was that this woman was weeping because she had not opened her heart, and with this thought, she was suddenly, shockingly, back in her chair in the library, the image of Mary before her.

Her immediate thought was negative: "Did I just see me? Am I the crying old woman?"

But the totality of the experience was bigger, more, and she knew something important had happened to her. She slowly got up from her chair to see if she was alright. She felt fine. The room still looked the same. She felt reassured and excited.

Questions began to rush through her brain:

"Did I actually go upward?" It absolutely felt that way.

" ... There is a light
whose glory Makes the
Creator visible to the
created mind ... "

"Why didn't I hit the ceiling?" No understanding.
"Did I just meet God?" No understanding.
"Was that real?" Absolutely. It was powerfully real.
"Where did I go?" No understanding.

She sat down again and remained very still. All of her agony over Poland, over being a woman in a man's world, being a person apart, hating her religion, her difficult adjustment to another culture, the strict demands she put on herself—all were gone. All that remained was love without an object. All there was, was unity.

At one moment in Paradise when the Pilgrim sees "a living light" in which there is "a glow of translucent substance bright, so bright, that my poor eyes could not endure the sight," he turns to Beatrice for help, and she tells him:

That which overcomes you now
has strength against which nothing has defense.
In it dwells the wisdom and the power
that opens the road between heaven and earth.

The Pilgrim then tells us what happened to him as he faced the light:

My mind began to swell until it broke its bounds
and what became of it, it does not know.

Beatrice sees that he has surrendered to the light, that the candle (his mind) is prepared for the flame (a taste of enlightenment), and, as his teacher, she gives him "an invitation that can never be erased from the book of my life."

Open your eyes, look straight into my face.
Such things have you been witness to that now
you have the power to endure my smile.

Christina had endured the power of Mary's wise, compassionate smile.

Ruth, Christina, and the others we have mentioned in this book, as well as we and you, are all pilgrims in this world. We all get lost and we all carry our weight, our form of hell, as well as the weight the world puts on us, around with us. Despite these conditions, we have the undeniable feeling of a promise in us, and you can see in all of our lives the search for the fulfillment of that promise. We have guided you on this journey to show you a path to that fulfillment, and we thank you for having traveled with us.

Michelangelo's Eyes

The courtyard of the Museo dell'Opera del Duomo (the museum of the Cathedral) is where Michelangelo sculpted his masterpiece, the marble statue of David. When it was finished in 1507, David turned out to be seventeen feet tall. The townspeople had to break down the front wall of the courtyard so that David could be wheeled on a cart through the streets of Florence to the Piazza della Signoria. In 1834, the statue was moved to the Galleria dell'Accademia on Via Ricasoli, where it is today.

David is a magnificent and unforgettable work of art, an event in your life. You cannot see him and not be changed. When you then realize that Michelangelo was an audacious twenty-seven-year-old when he completed David, amazement turns to incomprehension. You can understand only that such inspiration and genius are mysteries and that, really, the unknown world of potential inside each of us is a mystery, too.

Dante had helped us to go deeper into the mystery. Assagioli had helped us. Through his work and his methods, we had had many direct experiences of our own inner wisdom, our own Beatrice. We had learned how to listen to her in our professional work, in our personal life, in the choices we made about our life's direction, and we had come to believe that everyone's birthright of inner wisdom is the link to the greater truth of who we are and why we are here.

We walked into the Museo dell'Opera del Duomo thinking of Michelangelo. On the first floor stand tall, grim statues of Biblical prophets and then, around the corner, a magnificent moment of pure Italian humor—a huge statue of a seated Pope Boniface VIII (the Pope who betrayed Dante) at the end of the room with a "Men's Toilet" sign right next to him. Some Dante-lover had definitely been involved in choosing just the right spot for Boniface.

Halfway up the staircase to the second floor, there is a niche that holds a life-size statue of several people joined together. It is a Pieta, a depiction of Mary holding her dead son. Jesus is big and muscular, and his dead weight is pulling Mary down.

We sat down on a cool marble bench within the niche and studied the Pieta more closely. Behind Mary and Jesus are two other figures. One is Mary Magdalene. The other, towering above everyone, is Michelangelo as an old man.

Michelangelo sculpted himself into this Pieta. There he is, trying to hold up Mary, who is being pulled down by her heavy, dead son. You can feel them all sinking down from the weight of Jesus, sinking down from the weight of the suffering in the world, and old Michelangelo is straining to hold it all up.

His eyes seem dreamy, far away. He stares off into the distance, looking for something, or perhaps thinking of his own death. But he is still trying to help. He is trying to keep suffering from pulling everyone down.

We leaned back on the bench and felt the coolness of the stone. We looked at Michelangelo, and looked at Michelangelo, and looked at Michelangelo. Thoughts floated through our mind, but they were insubstantial, unimportant. We felt impelled to stay quiet and to keep our eyes on Michelangelo's eyes and not turn away, never turn away, no matter what.

- **Assagioli, Roberto**. The Act of Will, New York: Viking Press, 1973.

- **Assagioli, Roberto**. Psychosynthesis, New York: Penguin Books, 1976.

- **Assagioli, Roberto**. Transpersonal Development: The Dimension Beyond Psychosynthesis, Forres, Scotland: Smiling Wisdom, 2007.

- **Musa, Mark** (Editor and Translator). The Divine Comedy: Inferno, Indiana University Press, 1971.

- **Musa, Mark** (Editor and Translator). The Divine Comedy: Purgatory, Indiana University Press, 1981.

- **Musa, Mark** (Editor and Translator). The Divine Comedy: Paradise, Indiana University Press, 1984.

- **Schaub, Richard & Schaub**, B.G. The Florentine Promise: A Seekers Guide, Huntington NY: Florence Press, 2014. www.FlorencePress.com

- **Schaub, Richard & Schaub**, B.G. Transpersonal Development: Cultivating the Human Resources of Peace, Wisdom, Purpose and Oneness, Huntington NY: Florence Press, 2013. www.FlorencePress.com

- **Schaub, Richard & Schaub**, B.G. Transpersonal Development for Health and Well-Being: A Three CD Series of Meditations. Huntington NY: Florence Press, 2013. www.FlorencePress.com

- **Schaub, Richard & Schaub**, B.G. The End of Fear: A Spiritual Path for Realists, Carlsbad, California: Hay House, Inc., 2009.

- **Schaub, Bonney & Schaub**, R. Healing Addictions: The Vulnerability Model of Recovery, Albabny NY: Delmar, 1997.

- **John Coltrane**, Ole, Atlantic Jazz, 1989. As Dante did with words, Coltrane tried to force music to express the inexpressible. The title song, Ole, is the best fifteen minutes of emotional-spiritual music in history.

- **Donovan**, Sutras, American Recordings, 1996. The gentle, deep, vibrating voice of a spiritual seeker singing his own songs with acoustic back-up.

- **Ghazal**, Lost Songs of the Silk Road, Shanachie Records, 1997. Persian and Indian musicians bring together the longing and joy of two deep musical cultures steeped in spirituality.

- **Jim Goodin**, Celtic Journey to the Path, WoodandWireMusic@ hotmail.com, 1999. We wrote most of this book listening over and over again to this flowing solo acoustic guitar synthesis of American folk, blues, Indian raga, and Celtic melody.

- **George Harrison**, All Things Must Pass, EMD/Capitol, 1970. The Beatles brought Eastern spirituality to public attention, and Harrison's spiritual sincerity heard in such songs as "Hear Me Lord" is the universal longing to have the direct experience of God.

- **Hilliard Ensemble**, In Paradisum, 2000, ECM Records. This is one example of how music itself can meditate for you and bring you into higher states of awareness.

- **Keith Jarrett**, Changeless, ECM Records, 2000. Trance music of transparent joy.

- **Van Morrison**, Astral Weeks, Warner Bros., 1968. Without exaggeration, we have listened to this recording thousands of times and still love every note of it.

- **Van Morrison**, Common One, Warner Bros., 1980. The most overtly spiritual of Van's recordings, he finds a way to articulate the inarticulate speech of the heart.

- **Steve Reich**, Music for Eighteen Musicians, Nonesuch Records, 1997. People either absolutely love or absolutely hate this recording. It is quiet, shimmering trance music that can evoke higher states of awareness just by focusing on it.

- **Mike Scott**, Bring 'em All In, Chrysalis/EMI Records, 1995. A Scots rocker, former leader of The Waterboys, he chronicles his spiritual journey in very moving, persuasive terms with just voice and guitar.

- **Sequentia**, Canticles of Ecstasy: Hildegard von Bingen, 1994, Deutsche Harmonia Mundi. The Medieval mystic Hildegard wrote this music to take you into higher consciousness, and the proof of its effectiveness is that when several of our patients with chronic pain listened to this recording, they had no pain and were taken to a place of mental peace.

- **Staples Singers**, The Gospel According to the Staples Singers, Dressed to Kill, 1999. The emotional and spiritual intensity of this family of gospel musicians is unrivaled joy and sorrow.

ACKNOWLEDGMENTS

We gratefully acknowledge all of our patients, clients, and students through the years who have opened their minds and hearts to us and helped us to understand so much more than our own limited experience could have shown us. The exchange of energies between you and us has sustained us many times over.

We offer a special acknowledgment to George Schaub, an internationally respected photographer and author of twenty books on photography. He generously opened his studio and files to us in our search for this book's imagery.

We also acknowledge our design team at Aericon – Dean, Sam, and their colleagues. It's a pleasure to work with you.

CPSIA information can be obtained at www.ICGtesting.com
Printed in the USA
LVOW10s1932061015

457167LV00020B/222/P

9 780692 276853